Echoes From a Small Town... a Long Time Ago

Enjoy!

from Kay + Perry Savage

Home
is a place you grow up wanting to leave,
and grow old wanting to get back to.

John Ed Pearce

Tim H. Webb

ISBN 13: 978-1-945976-03-2

Published by EA Books Publishing a division of
Living Parables of Central Florida, Inc. a 501c3
EABooksPublishing.com

DEDICATION

Dave Ardoin

This book is dedicated to Dave Ardoin, a friend and colleague who left us way too soon. Dave was a Cajun, born and raised in Louisiana, and he wore it proud. Dave was a graduate of the University of Louisiana at Lafayette. There has never been a more avid fan of the "Ragin Cajuns."

Dave introduced me to the Cajun's tailgate and all manner of Cajun food. One of my proudest moments was when he commissioned me an "adopted" Cajun.

Dave was one of the kindest and most benevolent people I have ever known. I am a better man for having been his friend. Love you, man! Until we meet again, *"Laissez les bons temps rouler."*

ACKNOWLEDGEMENTS

I would like to thank those who encouraged me to compile these stories and saw the book to its fruition. Thank you!

To Kathy Webb, for being my cheerleader and proofreader. You have always made me smile and I love you more each day.

To Louisa Jeffries, who was so wonderful to work with as the copy editor of this work. Any errors that may be found were entered by me after her job was finished.

To Ken Grissom, Ken Studdard and Phronsie Owens for the old photographs they shared. The picture of the train on the back cover is credited to Myrtle Pierce, Phronsie's grandmother, who lived on Seaboard Avenue. It is inscribed with the year 1969-Silver Comet, as the last passenger train to pass through Piedmont. It was taken from the front yard of her home.

To my daughter, Brooke Vakakes, for her computer literacy and never losing her patience while trying to teach an "old dog" like her dad. 5th grade teachers have to develop that skill.

To Kathy Snead, a high school classmate, for writing the Foreword. Kathy received a B.S. from Judson College, and her Masters from West Georgia College. She has an amazing singing voice and boundless energy. Kathy has directed so many theater productions, the list is longer than this book!

To Danny Beavers, who assisted me in tracking down old addresses, original names and drove me around town on my visits so I could take notes.

To James Cartee, for his expertise and guidance through the publishing process.

TABLE OF CONTENTS

FOREWORD

Back in the '50's and early '60's, in addition to segregated races, boys and girls were pretty much segregated by sex, although we did interact in school and church. And, that is exactly where I first met Tim, at Piedmont First Baptist Church. There we participated together in Sunday School, Training Union, Church Services, Vacation Bible School, Bible Sword Drills, Easter Egg Hunts, Church Camp, etc. Tim and I were friends, but would have undoubtedly been even closer had it not been for the letters T, U, V.

While Tim and the guys were busy with hunting, fishing, Boy Scouting, football, baseball, and racing events, we girls were out selling those Girl Scout cookies, taking piano lessons, singing, etc. At the time, I didn't know that when Tim missed church on Sunday that he was at the race track! Yikes! Some considered that the behavior of heathens! But, not true of our Tim. He was well liked by everyone. And, why shouldn't he be? He was handsome, friendly, studious, and popular. Well, he was a radio DJ, for goodness sake. AND, he had a groovy Mustang!!!

In high school, Tim and I double dated a lot. We all had the best times, being silly, laughing, parking, riding the regular route through town, from the Dari King at the top of the hill through town, turning right on North Center Avenue, circling the Coffee Cup Cafe and repeating, oh, at least twenty times a night while singing those Beatle and Bee Gees' tunes. I can hear us now singing, "I Wanna Hold Your Hand" "Help!" and "To Love Somebody." Ah, the good old days.

Through the years, I've consistently stated that our childhoods in Piedmont were idyllic. We didn't lock our car doors and sometimes slept with unlocked house doors. Life was certainly centered around church, family and school. We didn't have electronics, but, did take typing in Mrs. Naugher's class (stop laughing kids). We watched little television, as we only had three

v

channels. Our girl's sleepovers were spent dancing, eating, singing and giggling about Tim, that Mustang, and all the other guys in school. I don't believe boys had spend the night parties, did they?

As adults, Tim, and his wife Kathy, continued pursuing Tim's childhood interests. In addition to Nascar, he has a love for writing and credits his teacher, Mrs. Jennings, for encouraging this talent. At age 9, he was asked to read a poem at church that he authored. That moment may have inspired his continued desire to write. In fact, he has written a book you should read. Oh, right...that is THIS book.

Another interest that we share as adults is our love of history. Tim and his wife Kathy enjoy traveling and annually venture to Europe with friends. Tim has also pursued his love of the Civil War period by reading an enormous amount of the history, as well as going on Civil War expeditions, with renown historians, to the Southeastern part of the country. Tim is well versed in Civil War history and I have hopes that, one day, he will go back to Piedmont and speak on this subject to his hometown friends.

In addition to his successful career, beautiful children, and grandchildren, Tim and Kathy opened their home to Tim's mother and to his now quadriplegic older brother Mike. Mrs. Webb passed away a few years ago, but Tim, Kathy and a caregiver continue to provide excellent care to his brother.

I would be remiss not to mention Tim's outstanding parents. They had three children and did a wonderful job raising each one. Tim's dad seemed to be a man of few words. But, I bet Tim, Kay, and Mike were attentive when he did speak. Their parents ensured that their children grew up with strong Christian values and professional standards. The entire family dressed very well, had a beautiful home, and, as expected, were well spoken and had excellent manners. And, those attributes had a lot to do with Mrs. Webb. What I remember most about her is her smile and how impeccably she dressed. I never saw her without her makeup and hair perfectly done. She kept a lovely home and showed much love to her husband and children. She was an extremely friendly, lovely lady and I'm sure is greatly missed by her family.

Now back to these letters T, U, and V. How are these letters relevant to our friendship? Our seating charts for each classroom were alphabetized by last names... mine began with "S" and Tim's with "W." Aha!! So, those T, U, and V students prevented us from whispering in class, but, we perfected passing notes.

What else is there to say about Tim? He is full of passion for life, for his family, friends, travel, history, reading, writing, good wine, and memories of his childhood. I can see my friend Tim now, seated in his gorgeous garden, sipping his favorite wine, classical music softly playing, all whilst reminiscing...with a contented smile on his face.

Kathy Snead

PROLOGUE

My wife, Kathy, and I often discuss technology we've been exposed to in the last thirty years – all the things we never had access to as teens and even as young adults. Like most everything in life, there is the good and the bad. So many people today, everywhere you look, have their noses deep in a screen. Kids are lost without their iPads. Personal face-to-face conversation is taking a back seat to our devices.

It warmed my heart recently to see several kids on the floor of my local bookstore, reading. Don't get me wrong, I love the fact that I can instantly look up a word on my electronic dictionary or Google how to fix my leaking faucet. I enjoy reading my Bible on my phone, but sometimes I just become overwhelmed with the intrusions technology has brought into my life. Seventy-five percent of the bills we pay for services and products each month were not even available to the last generation. Those of us born in the '50s through the '70s didn't have the many things that bombard us today and demand our time. We actually had to go shopping at the store. We had to use a landline phone, many with party lines. We used the U.S. Postal Service to send letters and could only listen to music on the radio or stereo at home. We had to go to the box office to buy tickets for concerts and the theater. Our text was a handwritten note handed to our girlfriends as we passed in the hallway at school.

My first year at the University of Alabama, I had to use a slide rule for calculations. My children probably wouldn't know what a slide rule is. The next year, I paid $150 for one of those new handheld calculators I can buy today for a few bucks.

I love our modern conveniences, but like many people, I strongly dislike the way they tether us to anyone who wants our time. They can intrude on me anywhere and anytime, without my consent. Some days I just want to get away, back to a simpler time when the pressures of life were still far away and my world seemed so small.

I grew up in Piedmont, Alabama. It was a mill town of about 5,000 people. To a young boy, the city limits were the limits to his universe. A few years back I received a copy of letters my grandmother wrote home to my mom while living away in Denver, Colorado, for a time. Those letters gave me a glimpse into her life I had never known. I was fascinated by her description of everyday life, chores, worries and challenges. It was at that time I started to write a personal journal. I've recorded my life there for almost 30 years. I thought someday my grandchildren and their children might enjoy reading about my life and times before they knew me. I also began to write down stories and essays of memories of my childhood in Piedmont. It gives me great joy to recount those times and record them. It is a sort of respite from the business of everyday life now. I'm transported back to happy times and old friends I have lost touch with, to unique places and people. The mischievousness of a young boy is explored in an environment that no longer exists.

I began to share these stories with friends. I was encouraged to publish them in a book.

Friends from other parts of the country told me they could relate to the same things I remembered from my childhood. Their childhood mimicked mine in many ways. Those who shared these times in Piedmont also encouraged me. This book is the result.

I have so enjoyed reliving these stories in compiling this volume, though my wife says she wishes she had known some of this before she married me! My hope is that it will rekindle your past in a similar way. I try to write in such a way as to transport you there; I want you to feel and smell the place, hear the people talk, see their scars, feel the numbing coldness of a stream in the forest, or your clothes clinging to your body from perspiration on a sweltering day in August. My wish, too, is to honor those who molded me growing up. You will meet many of them here. We should all record our memories, for they are all our kin will have of us someday.

Tim H. Webb

July 25, 2018

1

Coming of Age

****

The sultry days of summer send me tripping back through the cobwebs of my dimming memory to those carefree days of long ago coming of age in Piedmont, Alabama, my childhood home.

Mornings were often spent at the library in the old high school on North Main Street. Mrs. Johnson, the librarian, was always present, ready to recommend a book.

There was no air conditioning as I recall, but it was always cool there, sitting at one of the large library tables, pockmarked with the initials of a bored student who had marred it with his graffiti during a study hall period long ago.

The tall windows yawned open to admit the cool morning breeze as I read in the shadows of the book stacks. That must be the place I developed my love of reading. I still remember one of those titles, "No Moon on Graveyard Head." Sitting beneath buzzing fluorescent lights, books took me to places I could only dream of. I'm still mesmerized by the small wooden drawers that held the card catalog. The cards all had holes in the bottom through which a large metal rod passed, I suppose so no one would remove the cards. Stacks of scrap paper littered the top of the card catalog cabinet, conveniently placed there so one could record the information on the card and then wander through the stacks to find that which they sought. Today, computers rob us of that experience, the glory of finding that for which you look without electronic assistance.

The old wooden floors, swept so many times they had a dull red patina, creaked like an old wagon when students passed through.

Mornings at the library gave way to afternoons at the YMCA. At that time, the YMCA had the only public pool in town. Later the City Pool would open on the other end of town. Mr. Clyde Pike was the mayor of the Y. Actually, I am not sure what his title was, but for the kids in Piedmont who flocked there, he was the mayor of that domain. He sat on a tall stool behind the counter and knew the name of every child who entered. He wore a large ring of keys on his belt, each fitting a different lock or door in the cavernous building.

The gym doubled as a skating rink on Friday and Saturday nights. Many a "first love" sprouted there in the dim lights, amid the roar of skates and the loud rock music that engulfed us.

Mr. Pike issued basketballs for pickup games in the gym. The windows of the gym were covered in wire curtains, large metal screens that hung like doors over the glass to protect them from an errant basketball, yet allowed light through the dusty panes. He parceled out Ping-Pong balls and paddles for the table by the window that looked out on the pool. Checkers were available for those so inclined. The checkers were bottle caps; one side used tops up, the other used bottoms up. When no one else was around to play you, Mr. Pike would be the foe. I never saw him lose a game of checkers, and I am sure I saw him play hundreds of times.

The interior of the Y was always redolent of old leather furniture and a musty gym. There were vending machines that would distribute Grapico, Orange Crush and RC Cola, all in heavy glass returnable bottles. I can still see the water condensing on the bottle in the heat of a summer's day. A large wire rack sat next to the vending machine where you placed your empty bottles for the vendor to pick up.

Swimmers would be issued a wire basket from the locker room. You took your basket to a changing area, deposited your clothes in the basket and then returned it to the locker attendant. Each basket was numbered and had a large brass safety pin attached to it with its corresponding number. The safety pin was removed from the basket and pinned to your bathing suit, quite an effective system of keeping track of patrons clothing.

The path from the locker room to the pool took you through a shallow wading pool. I suppose it was some sort of disinfectant. The pool had both a high and low diving board. Public pools today would never allow this. Our society has become much too litigious. Back then people took responsibility for their own actions. The water was always so inviting, a brilliant blue, reflecting the sun from its painted cement bottom.

Nights after supper you would hear the banging of screen doors all over the neighborhood as kids raced outside into the coming darkness. Now it was time for "cops and robbers", a sort of combination of tag and hide- and- seek played on bicycles. We would race along the sidewalk on South Main, dodging the mounds of cement that had erupted when the roots of the large oak trees that lined and shaded the street pushed them up. We'd cross the tracks of the Seaboard and then, just a few blocks away, the Southern railroad and then zip through the deserted streets of downtown, on to the lower end and the mill village. I still recall the essence of hot machinery and cotton thread from Standard Coosa Thatcher, locally known as the cotton mill. The redolence permeated the air and would waft over the town at night.

Sometimes we would ride the back alleys, those convenient little chert roads behind every house used primarily by garbage trucks for trash pickup. Today we have to roll our cans to the street on garbage pickup days. Back then, large 55-gallon drums sat behind most every house where trash was either burned or picked up by the garbage truck. Our modern neighborhood doesn't even have back alleys.

Bikes would turn into cars as we entered those teen years that brought new adventures. Those same cars would take many of us away, some to college, others to serve their country or seek jobs in larger cities. Some never returned. Others never left.

Sometimes late at night, my mind wanders back to those carefree days of my youth and the innocence and safety of a time long past. Often, on a stressful day in the city, I long to go back to those times, if only for a day. It isn't meant to be. Oh, I can go back to the town, but it isn't the same. That town, those people, that time, are long past, but they still shape who I am.

Tim H. Webb

YMCA

Cotton Mill

Piedmont High

2

Dugger Mountain

****

Since I left Piedmont, Alabama in the early '70's, I have had the opportunity to travel to the far reaches of the United States, the Baltics and to much of eastern and western Europe. There are so many beautiful sites I've witnessed in those travels.

On a recent visit back to Piedmont, I was reminded that God did not leave this little hamlet out when he spread his beauty.

Have you ever stood atop Highland Cemetery out on the 278 ByPass, especially in the spring or fall, and looked out across Piedmont? The image is fairy-tale like; the town spread out below. In the spring, it is idyllic, all dressed in deep green; you can even see furrows from the gardens, the dark rich soil like a part in the land. In the fall, you may see tendrils of leaf smoke from burning piles of leaves at the side of the street. There may be an ordinance against that now, but it was once so. It seems so unhurried; no impatient car horns if someone sits too long at a green light. The town stretches south to where it nestles up against Dugger Mountain. These are the foothills of the Appalachians, the birthplace of the rugged range that runs all the way up the eastern side of the U.S., ending in the state of Maine.

Drive out of town south on Main Street until it unwinds into Highway 9. Just a few miles from the curve, Dugger Mountain pops up again to the southeast, majestic; not like the Rockies mind you, but just as masculine in a smaller way. The mountain girds the highway on your left all the way through Nances Creek.

There is a stretch of road here that runs straight and flat for just over a quarter of a mile; we called it the Walnut Tree, eponymously named for an old growth tree that towered over the end of this stretch of road. The Walnut Tree was often the site of un-ordained drag races late at night. The sound of those deep throated and un-muffled engines would reverberate off the mountains on either side of the highway, then thunder back at you a split second later in an echo. These were the days before unleaded fuel, when four-barrel carburetors still aerated the engine and seatbelts had yet to debut.

If you exit Highway 9 just south of town and take the Babbling Brook Road toward Vigo, you get an entirely different view, this one closer and more intimate, but just as soothing to the soul. Just past the Catholic church, a tiny farm road falls away to the right and follows the banks of the creek. The creek is now straight and clean. Back in the day it would twist and turn through the pastures and woods, choked occasionally with whatever kinds of plants like to grow up from the streambed. Cane breaks were common. This road once led to a horse farm owned by the family of a friend of a friend. We often came here late in the day to ride horses along the fence line that hugged up close to the base of the mountain. As the sun began to set, we would drive back along that narrow road and park beneath the tall trees that lined the creek bank where we would drink bootlegged beer sitting on the hood of the car while the raucous sound of Credence Clearwater Revival's "Green River" belted

8

from the radio.

Back out on Babbling Brook Road, you can hang a right and drive through Vigo. The verdant pastures along the way are populated with healthy livestock. Cattle share the pastures with old abandoned farm equipment. The skeletal remains of an old tractor lies drunkenly on its side, one large rear wheel forever missing, probably salvaged for parts, the other having lost its rubber tire sinks into the fertile loam. On a hill, a bleached barn leans aslant in the afternoon sun, which escapes the withered boards and forms strange shadows on the ground. The tin roof of the barn is ambered with rust from years of acid rain. If the car window was down, and it usually was, as only the Bourgeoisie owned air-conditioned cars in those days, you'd smell the sweet hay that had been cut and baled earlier in the day. One of the hardest jobs I ever had, as a boy here, was the summer I hired on to load bales of hay onto a tractor pulled wagon. The tractor went slow but never stopped. We would toss the bales up to another worker on the wagon who stacked them. You had to hurry to keep up with the creeping tractor. The bales were heavy and the hay would mangle your arms and you'd itch for a week. I recently saw a tractor loading the hay all by itself. There was a large projection on the front of the tractor like a huge metal spike. The spike would be run into the end of the bale, then lifted on to the wagon. Somehow, that seems like cheating.

Up ahead you pass the entrance to Hanks Cemetery, a lover's lane of sorts in my adolescence. I can still remember driving around the circular road, what are now classic cars leaning off the shoulder in the moonlight, windows fogged from the activity with-in. If you were looking for a buddy on Saturday night and couldn't find him in town, you'd drive up and around Hanks to see if maybe he'd gotten lucky.

Just past Hanks you would hang a right and drive to a fork in the road where another right would soon find the pavement giving way to dirt, the familiar sound of the tiny rocks peppering the undercarriage of the car. Here you started the climb up the near face of the mountain. Just a mile or so ahead, a smaller road turned off to the right. A small indiscreet wooden sign shaped like an arrow said "Dugger Tower."

For some time, we had been intrigued by the slim silver obelisk we watched each afternoon reflecting the last vestiges of the setting sun atop the mountain. At night, its blinking red light could be seen for miles. Seeing it up close became an obsession. One summer's day, a friend and I persuaded an older neighbor who had a driver's license to take us up there.

When we turned off on the tower road, our path suddenly became narrow. It swelled and weaved itself through the forest for what seemed like ages until we finally emerged on the crest of the mountain. Towering above us was the fire tower, appearing much larger up close. It reached into the sky for what seemed like forever, appearing to get smaller toward the top. We began our climb up the switchback stairs, fearing to look down after a few stories. As we rose up the tower's staircase, the wind began to tug at us, we gripped the handrails tighter and slowly inched our way to the top. Suddenly we arrived at the floor of the tower house. A knock, and the ranger inside lifted the heavy wooden door in the floor to allow us inside.

The glass tower house smelled of cigarette smoke and cedar pencil shavings. The ranger inside was a bit gruff, but seemed somewhat glad to have the company. He wore khaki pants over thick boots. His shirt was full of pockets and he wore a forest green ball cap style hat with a U.S. Forest Service emblem on the front. His beard was unkempt. Just beneath the tall glass windows were shelves that contained tools of the trade. The binoculars the ranger would look through every few minutes were the largest I had ever seen, a beat-up metal lunch box and a thermos stood nearby. A round table in the center of the room was covered with maps and instruments for determining exact locations and distances.

The ranger was vigilant. His eyes rarely focusing on us as he talked, constantly scanning the horizon for a sign of smoke. A government issued radio rattled in the background, his only form of communication with the outside world.

The panorama that greeted us through the windows was breathtaking. I had not yet flown in an airplane, but when I did years later it reminded me of this view. Piedmont looked like a toy village off to the northwest, the roads spreading out across the countryside were like wispy ribbons winding through the low hills. The cars appear as tiny insects as they inched along. You could see all the way to Weiss Lake over in Cherokee County. We didn't stay long. We knew if we tarried, we would be asked to leave. After all, we were intruding into the ranger's work place. It was important that he stay focused on the job at hand.

Back at the base of the tower, I was glad to be back on solid ground. I now had a different perspective on the place I lived. I realized how small and insignificant I was in the big picture. Driving back to town I couldn't help but think about how lonely a job that ranger had, sitting up there in the sky all alone for days on end. I know I would feel close to God up there. I wonder if he did?

Many years later when I was home from college one summer, I rode a motorcycle back up that road. The tower had long since been disassembled, gone from the horizon, no longer needed. Its metal skeleton is probably rusting away in some junkyard in another county; or maybe its mass has been melted into something else more useful. The ranger had been replaced by some more efficient means of monitoring the forest for fires.

The road was unkempt and gutted by years of flooding, it no longer needed to be navigable. After a few hundred yards, I was forced to turn back. The road became impassable. The rich green pine forest that once grew close to the road had been cut; scrub brush grew in its place and displaced the road in places. It seemed that this place was irreparably scarred.

As I tend to do when I see the past has faded away and something new has taken its place, I wondered what happened to the ranger who worked there. I could imagine the day he was told that he was no longer needed. He was replaced by a machine or a satellite or some other creation of modernity; faster, more efficient, cheaper.

I guess it is the natural progression of things that more efficient things replace them. Change is inevitable. With each one, a little piece of Americana dies. I realize these things certainly make life easier for us. They increase profits or reduce cost. Somehow, they seem more sterile. They certainly take away the fun.

Tim H. Webb

Dugger Mountain

3

Once Upon a Time

****

While visiting a movie theater recently in a mega complex with sixteen plus movies showing at the same time, I was reminded of how having too many choices complicates life.

I grew up in Piedmont, Alabama, where the Allison Theater was the only option for a movie within 25 miles, if you didn't count the drive-in on the outskirts of town, and I didn't, because it opened and closed with regularity. Besides, you couldn't walk or ride a bike to the drive-in.

The Allison sat on Center Avenue between the First National Bank, a stately white building with an ornate black wrought iron fence bordering a neatly manicured lane of grass just inside the fence and McClellan's Five and Dime on the other side. Just south of there was the Little Gem Café, once owned by my grandparents but now run by the Payne family. A back alley separated the Little Gem from the train depot, which stood hard by the Seaboard Railroad. Across the street from the theater was the Gurley James Furniture store. I am sure the theater was eponymously named but was owned at the time by the Woolf family, Evelyn and

Arnold, who happened to be my aunt and uncle.

It cost a dime to see the movie. My dime would often come sliding back to me with my ticket as I stretched to reach the small window behind which sat my aunt, with a smile on her face. I guess that was one of the perks of being related to the owner. It also increased the bounty I had to spend at the concession counter, which greeted you just inside the front doors with their opaque windows. Outside those doors was one of those ubiquitous weight scales of the day. You could stand on it, deposit a penny, and get your weight and your fortune. What a deal!

I loved the "sputnik", a drink made by Mrs. Parker, the attendant, by mixing a bit of every fountain flavor available in the same cup. It must have been named after the Russian satellites of the day.

I'd purchase a pack of "Charms", a candy similar to Life Savers, only square and without a hole in the middle. I remember once getting one of those things hung in my throat standing by the water fountain in the theater. An attendant, certain I was going to die, held me up by my ankles and shook me until the candy was expelled. I now know why they put holes in Life Savers.

Drink and candy in hand, I would enter the theater proper, the only one, through heavy red velvet drapes that hung across the entrances on either side of the concession counter. These elegant curtains would be tied back with thick, golden ropes at the beginning and the end of the movie to allow patrons to enter and exit, then closed during the movie to keep the auditorium dark by blocking out light from the lobby.

Once inside, you would find a row to slip into. Your Keds would stick to the floor as you walked to your seat, the result of years of spilled fountain drinks. No cup holders on these utilitarian seats! There was a balcony above the auditorium that was accessed through a door to the left of the main entrance out front. The door was marked "Colored." The "coloreds" had no access to the concession counter but could ask the ticket seller to get them refreshments and deliver them through the ticket window when they were not busy with other duties. We just accepted that back then. It is shameful to me today.

To access the men's room, you had to climb a flight of stairs covered in thick, crimson carpet on the right side of the lobby. Once there, a large window opened out onto the street below. It seemed the roof of the marquee that hung out over the sidewalk was always littered with refuse thrown from the window by mischievous boys. I loved to stand in that window after the movie and just watch the traffic pass below. The projection room was next to the men's room and could be entered through a narrow door a few steps up a staircase from the men's room. Red Smith was always on duty there, except when he was racking balls at the pool hall up the street. Cecil Parris was another employee who was always kind to the smaller kids. I think he later became a city policeman. I'm sure he was the one who saved me from choking on that "Charms" candy.

On Saturdays, a triple feature ran with seductive advertising like "Horror-o-Rama" or "War-o Rama." There often was a serial Western feature that continued from week to week, much like a television soap opera.

Leaving the theater on a bright, sunny afternoon, I would pause a moment beneath the marquee for my eyes to adjust to the light. While cars parked along the street, the curb immediately in front of the theater was reserved for bicycles; there would be a tangled mass of them there on a Saturday afternoon.

My trip home would take me by the Little Gem Cafe, then down an alley. There was a large exhaust fan from the kitchen of the Little Gem that blew out into the alley. Oh, the aroma of the spicy chili that would greet me there on my way home. At the end of the alley was the Kwik Chek grocery on Main Street. One day it became the Winn-Dixie and moved out on the bypass.

My dad was a friend of Mr. Thurman Young, the store manager of the Kwik Chek. I distinctly remember one New Year's Eve when friends were gathered at our house to welcome in the New Year. Sometime after midnight everyone wanted breakfast but we had no breakfast food in the house. Mr. Young and my dad, with me tagging along, went to the Kwik Chek where Mr. Young unlocked the door and we gathered breakfast items in the cavernous, dimly lit store. Two things still reside with me from that night, one being in the large store with low lights in the wee hours of the morning with no one else there. The other thing was that Mr. Young added up the cost of the food before we left and put the money for it on the ledge of one of the closed registers. I thought, "How honest of him", no one would have known he took the food, and, after all, he was the store manager. That made an impression on me.

From the Kwik Chek, I would take the railroad tracks the hundred or so feet to my house. Some days I would stop to browse the merchandise at Will Mauldin's What-Not Shop across the street from the grocery. Will sold lots of used machinery: lawn mowers, washing machines, bikes, saws and other rusty things that had been redeemed by Mr. Mauldin from some shed in the country and restored to working order. These things were scattered all over the dirt yard in front of the store, each with a small white tag attached by a string with its price, negotiable of course. The space was always neat. Folks like him who had lived through the Great Depression never threw anything away, "you might need it someday," and they had done without for far too long. My dad was the same way. When he died there were a couple of dozen coffee cans full of all manner of nuts and bolts, washers and nails, scattered about his basement.

On a recent trip back to Piedmont, it was saddening to see all the empty storefronts. None of the buildings I remembered remain the same. It is hard to tell where the old theater was. Dozens of storefronts look tired, their windows clouded over, "For Rent" signs hung precariously from the doors. There is one store still there that I remember from my childhood. Miraculously, "Strickland's" remains open. I guess in modern parlance it would be a hardware store. I think we called it a general store. You could buy anything from paint to pliers, from bikes to BB guns. I think the store is still run by the family of the original owner. God bless them. They cling to a way of life that has passed the rest of the town by. I hope they last. There once were a few other stores like it if you count the "Western Auto" run by Mr. Loftin and "Street and Mobbs" managed by Mr. Leo Street, just a few doors down on Ladiga Street.

I think Pope's City Barber Shop is still open, though I heard Curtis was viciously attacked not long ago by an irate person he had loaned money. Go figure. Curtis Pope's shop holds fond memories. Talk about the coolest thing you ever saw as a kid? Curtis had a rattlesnake, a huge coiled up thing with skin like an Indian blanket and beady eyes, but looked so alive. Of course, it had been stuffed by a taxidermist. It lay atop a cabinet prominently displayed in the waiting area of the shop. Curtis had the rattles on that snake wired some sort of way so that when an unsuspecting kid wandered close to take a look, he could flip a switch behind his barber chair and the snake would come alive, vibrations and rattles loud as a room full of maracas! Today you would probably be sued for such a stunt, but it sure was funny back then. As locals, we loved to take a new kid or visitor by the City Barber Shop to see the spectacle, then stand by and watch as they had the bejesus scared out of them.

It may seem silly but it pains me to see such a memorable place, where life began for me, erode away. It is hard to believe that at one time in the '60s there were four new automobile dealerships thriving in town. That was before interstate highways sucked away the traffic and the big box stores drew locals to bigger cities close by. The mills were still prosperous and would run overtime much of the year. All are shuttered now.

When leaving town, I drove by the old Lawtex building on 5th Avenue. It later became Springs, owned by a company in South Carolina. While in college, I spent a couple of summers working there. My mom was secretary to the plant manager for many years, so I know the place paid for much of my raising and education. The capacious building and its sister out on Highway 278 stand vacant, like some scene from Chernobyl, but from a different cause. Some blame it on NAFTA. The loading docks, where I once unloaded batting to be used in making quilted bedspreads and comforters, are dilapidated. Weeds nip at the perimeter of the building, and the fence that once surrounded the place lies precariously on its side.

Someone once said that the business of life is the acquisition of memories and in the end, that is all there is. Since leaving this place many years ago, I have traveled the world. I have visited many of the places I once read about in the school library here or studied in geography and history class. Those places created many memories, but none more precious or treasured than the ones created during my misspent youth in Piedmont, Alabama.

Allison Theater

Piedmont Drive-In

Kwik Chek Grocery

First National Bank

4

Mommie Pearl and the Trains

****

Piedmont, Alabama is a textile town, inhabited by modest, moral people who work in the mills, farm fertile loam in the foothills of the Appalachian Mountains, and raise hardy, ruddy-cheeked children.

I grew up in Piedmont in the 1950's and 1960's in a duplex next to my grandmother's house on Smith Street. We called her "Mommie Pearl." Mommie Pearl was widowed. She lived on meager savings from a restaurant and a grocery business she and my grandfather ran in hard times before.

Her husband died in 1958 while being treated for tuberculosis in a hospital in Denver, Colorado. After that, times were hard for Mommie Pearl. She made ends meet however she could. When cleaning out her house years later, I found six or eight cigar boxes full of customers grocery receipts that had been charged at their store but never paid.

She sold handcrafts and crocheted items she created to supplement her income. As a young boy, I would ride with her to Weiss Lake, a body of water near Centre created by backing up the Coosa River.

Sunny days would find us driving to the lake in her 1960 Plymouth. The car had a three speed manual transmission because that is what she learned to drive, and she didn't think she could master those new automatics that had no clutch!

We would park her car and walk along the side of the lake on the shoulder of the road, searching for the perfect piece of wood bobbing at the water's edge, often bleached gray by the Alabama summer sun. She could always spot them better than me. She would eye a piece of wood and I would scramble down the sharp slate rocks to retrieve the wet treasure, smoothed by months of drifting in the lake.

Back at home she would fashion this wood into flower arrangements, nailing pieces together, adorning them with artificial flowers, moss gathered from damp shady spots beneath aged pecan trees in her backyard and all sorts of colorful satin birds she would find at McClellan's Dime Store. Like most folks back then, she was very adept at using whatever was available to make what she needed. The arrangements sat all over the house and in shops around town. I remember people coming to her house to buy the handcrafts she made. She would beam with pride when she sold one, pleased to make a profit from her ability to make something beautiful from things that cost her nothing, which she mostly rescued after Mother Nature cast them off. Times were difficult, but you would have never known by the way she took care of me. She kept me days while my two older siblings were in school and both my parents worked.

Strange how certain things linger in your memory. There was an old smokehouse in her back yard. When you opened its creaking door, you were greeted by the pungency of old things: tools, discarded kitchenware, broken furniture that might be repaired or repurposed one day.

There was an old, large, wooden box that sat in a corner. I remember some sort of stencil on it that indicated it once contained some kind of munitions, probably brought home from the Anniston Army Depot by my dad. The box was about six feet long and three feet deep and wide. In the winter, the box was filled with fresh pork from a pig killing at my uncle's farm. Many a cold winter's morning I would accompany an adult to retrieve a piece of pork from the box where it was buried in salt. Back in the kitchen the salt would be washed away and the meat fried up for breakfast. I am not sure why the meat was kept there. We had refrigeration. I guess it was once a necessity that carried over. Our forefathers often preserved meat with salt, and it was just a tradition that hung on. I often wonder how many people might have died in those days from eating meat that spoiled from lack of refrigeration.

In the yard, next to the smokehouse, was an umbrella table where my grandmother would serve us her famous hamburgers. My brother still says they were the best burgers he ever ate. She would crisp the bun with butter in the skillet and add chopped shallots she gathered from the yard to the other garnishes atop the meat. Many were the days I sat at that aluminum table, shooing summer flies while I ate, drinking a cold Pepsi cola in a returnable bottle and watching the traffic pass on the highway out front.

Mommie Pearl's back yard was bordered by the Seaboard Railroad, whose twice-daily trains brought the outside world to Piedmont. Some of my earliest memories are of trains, the distant whistle announcing its coming, the shudder of the ground as it passed, and the clatter of the large steel wheels as they raced across the groaning ribbons of rail. We used to place pennies on the rails to be transformed into tissue-thin medallions of copper in large, irregular shapes by the passing trains. Kids raced to be the first to discover the booty in the gray slag rocks after the train had passed.

When train whistles would blow, my grandmother would beckon me from rooms that smelled of Ben-Gay and old furniture, across clean floors of yellowing linoleum squares to the kitchen window, which looked out onto the tracks. The kitchen was always warm and smelled of fresh brewed coffee, the kind that percolates in tin pots. In winter, rivulets of water would inch down the glass as the morning sun melted the frost from the night before. I would clamber upon a kitchen chair she carefully placed beneath the window to enable me to see and anxiously await the train, Mommie Pearl standing behind me. As the engine lumbered into view and quickly passed, the engineer would wave heartily; we'd then wait for the caboose and the scene to repeat itself.

Mommie Pearl was known up and down the line for her pecan pies. She would often meet the "Silver Comet" when it labored to a stop one block east of her house. Fresh baked goods were a gift for the conductor and the engineer. The friendships established over the years and the luscious baked goods must have indebted the trainmen to my grandmother. It was a rare train that passed that didn't give up jetsam from the engine and caboose windows to tumble into my grandmother's back yard.

One of my fondest memories is of the trinkets and treasures the railroad men would throw from the train for my grandmother. I'm sure those who run the railroad would not permit such activity today!

There would always be a newspaper tossed from the train. As soon as the train had thundered past and a quiet stillness came back over the morning I would rush to the yard to retrieve the package, a rolled-up newspaper from some distant city through which the train had passed earlier in the day or night. I was always eager to see from where the paper came, but more importantly, what treasure the trainmen had hidden inside. Sometimes it was a candy bar, or gum, or some other confectionary surprise, the papers with datelines of places like Charlotte or Atlanta.

Some years later Mommie Pearl married a gentleman who was a conductor on one of those trains, and they enjoyed many years together. As a young adult, I looked forward to visiting them and hearing stories of his early days working on the railroad, the adventure of it all. He had a hand-written note from General George Patton, thanking him for transporting his troops in Europe during the war.

Mommie Pearl died in 1988 while I was living in Miami, Florida. Kathy and I came home for a week to help mom and dad clean out her house a month or so after she passed. While up in the attic handing down boxes that had been stored there for many years, I spotted a cookie jar covered in dust. My heart raced as I remembered that jar from when I was a child. There was no mistaking it, it was made of black ceramic with tiny, colorful flowers painted on its side. It had a heavy black lid and handles on the side near the top. I often had wondered what happened to that jar.

The jar stood on Mommy Pearl's cabinet. It was always filled with delicious cookies. She made old fashion tea cakes and some sort of sugar cookie that was adorned with a pecan half from last winter's wind fall crop. As I recall, the tea cakes never made it to the cookie jar. For some reason, she kept them wrapped in a towel in the cabinet. My favorite were the oatmeal cookies, whose warm aroma would fill the house when she baked them, and stir a hunger in a boy as he entered the house after a fall afternoon of sand lot football. (The recipe follows this story.)

She had bequeathed to me some of her furniture; a dining room set she bought long ago that had been water-damaged in a fire at the Bennett-Knight Furniture Company. There was also a Duncan Phyfe sofa, so ornate with those sled-like runners for wooden legs. That sofa always sat in front of the living room window when I was a child. I used to ride the armrest on the sofa, pretending it was my horse when I was playing cowboys. I was reprimanded many times for that. Finally, after the armrest became thread-bare from my frolics, they gave up and just put a cloth protector over the damaged spot.

My dad and a cousin drove all the way to Miami from Piedmont to deliver the furniture to my wife and me in a pick-up truck. That furniture has moved with us two times since. We recently created a suite in our bedroom where the china cabinet is used as a bookcase and the sofa sits in an alcove of windows, looking out into a wooded area. I love having these important pieces from my childhood as a part of our bedroom suite. I often sit and just look at them and remember the happy times and all the generations of my family that enjoyed them.

The mills in Piedmont are shuttered now, and the trains no longer provide lifeblood to the city. The railroad tracks have been removed and the railroad right of way has become a biking trail. It seems the tiny town passed on with Mommie Pearl and the trains.

Still, every time I hear a lonesome train whistle, those carefree days rush back across my graying mind. I run to the kitchen window in my memory, rivulets of condensation stream down the glass in the frosty winter morning, and I remember Mommie Pearl and the trains.

Mommie Pearl's Crisp Oatmeal
Cookie Recipe

<u>Ingredients</u>

1 cup brown sugar

1 cup white sugar

1 cup shortening

2 large eggs

1 ½ cups oatmeal

1 cup coconut

2 cups all-purpose flour

1 tsp. baking soda

1 tsp. salt

1 tsp. baking powder

1 tsp. vanilla flavoring

<u>Directions</u>

Cream sugars and shortening together. Add eggs and beat with mixer. Mix oatmeal, coconut, baking soda, salt, baking powder and flour in separate bowl. Add this to egg mixture. Add vanilla. Mix all together and let chill a while, then form small balls. Place the balls on cookie sheet and bake in moderate oven of 350 degrees until brown. _Do Not Press Balls_, they will spread in oven and have a crinkle top. Yield: 48 cookies

Little Gem Café

Silver Comet's last trip through Piedmont

5

Terrapin Creek

****

As the suffocating heat and humidity reach their peak in August in Alabama, I long for those barefoot days long ago beside the rivers and streams that surrounded us in Piedmont, Alabama.

Terrapin Creek was a favorite. I understand there is a canoe center on the creek now where you can rent a canoe and travel leisurely down the creek to be picked up at a pre-arranged time and place, then be transported back to your vehicle. What we would have given for that concierge service back then.

Before we could drive we would have our parents drop us there in the morning at a place just off Highway 278 we called the water works, I think because there was some sort of pump station there that supplied water to a filtering station close by.

Trails were worn into the fertile soil and foliage for a long way up the creek to the north. We could fish a new spot all day if we didn't mind traversing the undergrowth and tolerating the insects. To the south of the water works the creek was choked with those green plants that grew in shallow areas. Then the cold, clear water slipped beneath a bridge that spanned Highway 278. I don't ever remember going south along the creek, too overgrown I guess. Maybe it was private property. We had great respect for rules back then, well, most of the time.

We always had live bait. Red worms or dough balls or chicken livers guaranteed we'd come home with a catfish or bream or some other perch I have yet to identify.

One summer, I started a worm bed in a washtub out behind our house. I carefully watered the soil and sprinkled cornmeal on top to nourish the creatures. I didn't know what I was doing. Oh, but if I had Google in those days! Within two weeks of stocking the tub with lively red worms I managed to exterminate the whole bunch. My first lesson in economics: Sometimes it is more economical to purchase the product than produce it. We also had artificial lures we learned about from *Field and Stream* magazine. The *Field and Stream* publication was read with reverence every month, thus it laid next to the Bible by my bedside. Oh, the stories of big-time game fish and wild animal hunts that would send my mind racing. Years later I would experience some of those adventures with like-minded friends, fishing for sail fish in Costa Rica and Guatemala, hunting bear in Alaska and Russian boar in Florida. It all began with those *Field and Stream* magazines in my bedroom on Montview Road.

Once we learned of a new lure "guaranteed" to have caught the biggest bass in field tests, we rushed to Street and Mobbs to purchase it with funds earned doing summer chores. Despite the claims, nothing seemed to break down the resistance of the small bass in the stream as well as a cheap white Shyster. The Shyster was a lure made from a tube of lead, my favorite painted white with black spots, a treble hook on one end and a spinning blade on the other. It wouldn't surprise me if several of those old rusty things still hang tangled in the branches that hugged the creek bank and canopied its flow through the countryside.

Strange, we never swam in the creek there that I can remember. There were other places to swim. This was reserved for fishing. There may be another reason we didn't swim there: the Snake Catcher. One lazy afternoon as we packed our gear and awaited our ride home, a young man a bit older than us arrived. He carried two thick cane poles with large treble hooks attached to their ends, but no monofilament line, which was the necessity of any fishing pole. He asked if we had seen any snakes along the creek that day. The only snake I had seen prior to that day on this creek was wrapped around my stringer of fish enjoying his dinner when I pulled it from the creek one afternoon.

When we asked the young man how he was going to fish without line on his poles, he told us the poles weren't for fishing; they were for snagging snakes! He then asked if we would like to see how it was done. We followed him quietly along the creek bank, down the same trails we had fished from earlier in the day. We walked very slowly and methodically. It wasn't long until he spotted the first snake, sunning itself on a limb that hung out over the creek. It took my friend and me awhile to spot it, blending in so well with its surroundings. He gently and slowly reached out toward the snake with his snare, worming it between branches and leaves. Once in position he quickly pulled the snare toward us, and the wriggling cottonmouth was soon writhing around the pole. We were so frightened we stood a safe distance away. He would dispose of the head of the snake, remove the still-twisting snake from the hook and move on to the next prey.

That day he taught us how to move slowly, stopping often, observing every limb inch by inch. To this day I can still walk along a stream and find snakes others can't see.

Just east of the water works on Highway 278, there was a large lake off to the right, surrounded by spreading pastures full of livestock. In the trees across the way, hidden from all but the most curious eye, was a large house. I came to know this place as the John B. Lagarde lake and ranch. I heard stories about Mr. Lagarde, how he was a big game hunter who traveled the world in his quest for trophy animals. I was told too that he had created a museum of sorts in the house on the lake outside Piedmont, where many of his game trophies were housed. One of the highlights of my junior year in high school was when our class took a field trip to the Lagarde house. A caretaker of the ranch escorted us through the house. I was awestruck!

Inside this house were dozens of large African game animals, fully preserved, many in a setting of their natural habitat. There was a staircase whose handrails were made of elephant tusk. In his office, behind his desk, was a large rock. Looming up over the gigantic rock was a polar bear; standing on its hind legs it appeared to be about 11 feet tall and peered down at you from behind the rock. A notation said the polar bear was the largest ever harvested up until that time. Polar bears were rarely hunted after 1968 due to laws governing the land on which they live.

Here in this house on the outskirts of my hometown were some of the largest animals ever harvested by hunters. These were the same animals I read about in *Field and Stream*. I was even more enthralled to have learned through my reading that polar bears were the deadliest of all bears when provoked. Here I stood by a world record in my hometown!

I later learned that John B. Lagarde was a savvy businessman who lived in Anniston. He made his fortune in the concrete block and ready-made cement business. He had the house outside Piedmont as a getaway and to display all his trophies. I was also told that he bankrupted several times but always worked hard to regain his wealth, a story that couldn't come true in many places outside the United States.

I don't hunt much anymore. I lost interest after seeing so many graceful animals forced out of their habitat by man's intrusion. I don't have a problem with those who do hunt, as long as they are ethical and abide by game laws.

Until a few years ago we had a house on Lake Martin that was bordered by a forest. I put tree stands and feeders there to attract wildlife. I never harvested an animal there. I did spend many a colorful fall afternoon perched high in a tree observing the deer and turkey feeding. Truth is, I don't think I could have shot one had I wanted to. Life is hard enough for them these days without having to compete with man for their home and food. I just watched them as their beauty and grace made the woods come alive. I don't mean to imply I am against hunting. The hunters I know are noble sportsmen. Many times, their efforts thin animal populations where overcrowding is decimating them and improves overall health of the wildlife.

We currently live in Vestavia Hills, Alabama, a suburb of Birmingham, that is rife with wild game. I often find deer feeding in our yard at night. Feral hogs sometimes enter the neighborhood from a wetland area nearby. One neighbor had his newly sodded yard completely plowed up by these animals. Coyotes have been spotted recently. People here fear for their small pets when left outside alone.

Again, it is not the animals' fault. We moved in on them. Our rapid growth of community has intruded on their habitat. They are being forced into smaller and smaller areas and their food sources are being depleted by urban sprawl.

I have heard of efforts being made to remove the animals by hiring marksmen with bow and arrow to stalk them at night. Having just returned from a trip to the northwestern plains and learning of the history of the Native Americans in that part of our

34

country, I can't help but compare what happened to the Sioux, Cheyenne and Crow Indians there to what is happening to the wildlife. It happened in the South too, with the expulsion of the Cherokee and Creek and many other tribes. White Europeans moved in, they took the land, and in fear of retaliation the indigenous people were moved to reservations. Poverty, alcoholism and poor self-image ensued, as many were not able to find rewarding or satisfying work on these reservations. I don't mean to grow political here, but it is a sad reflection on our society that continues to plague us.

This summer past, on a trip to Spain and Portugal, we learned how centuries ago the Christians, Jews and Muslims all lived together for hundreds of years in peace. They even shared each other's houses of worship on different days of the week. We can only hope that this type of love and tolerance will spring from the generations to come.

6

Lessons From Jackson

****

[Author's note: While this story took place after I left Piedmont, I had many dogs as a child in Piedmont that could generate such a story. I thought those of you who have loved a pet would appreciate it.]

"You picked the wrong puppy!" That is what my wife exclaimed as I came home from work a few weeks after my daughter and I brought home a loveable chocolate Lab. My daughter had been after me for over a year to get her a puppy. We already had a small peekapoo named B.J. I didn't understand the need for another one and I don't know why her heart was set on a chocolate Lab, but it was. She would leave pictures of cute Labs on my desk, in my car, places where I would see them and be affected. If you've seen Lab puppies, you know how adorable they are. My daughter, through her conniving persistence and pulling my strings, always seemed to win these battles. I eventually gave in to my daughter's wishes.

I found an ad for chocolate Lab puppies in the local paper, all sired and birthed by AKC registered dogs. I am not sure what the significance of that is, but I know it drives the price up. On

Saturday morning, we drove about an hour north of Birmingham to a farm in the countryside. It was a cool fall morning, as I remember. The slight chill in the air quickened our step, having just stumbled through another sweltering summer. Upon our arrival, a gentleman standing in the front yard met us. After greeting us, he pointed to a pen some 30 yards behind the house. He told us the puppies were there and left us to go and take a look.

As we approached the pen we could see a brown mass of fur all piled together by the fence. The puppies were all on top of one another napping, except for one. One puppy was on top of all the others jumping up and down, yapping as if to say, "Pick me! Pick me!" After observing the sleeping puppies and the one hyper one, we decided that Mr. Hyperactivity had the most personality of the bunch. Once Brooke picked him up, he began to lick her face and snuggle against her neck. It was over. We had our chocolate Lab. She named him Jackson.

So began our journey of fourteen years with our chocolate Lab and a season of my life when I would learn many valuable lessons from him. I had no idea what this ball of fire would teach me. He was all gangly and uncoordinated. His huge paws seemed half the size of his head. He had beautiful blue eyes that would capture your heart. His big, floppy ears completed the picture.

"You picked the wrong dog!" Kathy, my wife, had been on the internet, researching "How to choose a Lab puppy." Supposedly Brooke and I should have done our homework before choosing this dog. The article she commanded me to sit down and read described our dog as an "alpha male". He was rambunctious, into mischief, didn't mind, and eventually became jealous of me when I would show Kathy affection. If he saw me hugging her, Jackson would bound into the room and wedge himself between us. He never bit me, but I often felt threatened.

My wife's internet research was triggered by the fact that this mongrel was incorrigible. He chewed anything he could get his mouth around. If it was not fastened down, he would chew it and then hide it. If something edible was in a cabinet he could reach, he would claw at it until the wood was scratched and bare of paint. If you tried to pick him up during one of these forays, he would bite your finger with his tiny, razor like teeth. He would lurk near the front door and when an unaware family member or guest entered or left, he would escape outside, down the steps and off into the neighborhood, running hither and there to celebrate his newfound freedom and discover other ways to cause damage.

Since Brooke and I were gone during the day, Kathy was left to fend with this new member of the family. Thus, my wife's desperate internet search to discover all the mistakes we made when choosing our dog so she could remind us when we returned each day to hear of Jackson's misadventures. Through the trials of puppyhood, I learned the *lesson of patience.*

About the same time Jackson came to live with us, we bought a lake house about an hour away on Lake Martin. I remember the first time I took Jackson there. We had gone alone for a day or two away, and I was anxious to see if Jackson could swim. Of course, I knew Labs were water dogs, actually bred to retrieve wounded fish that escaped from the nets of Scandinavian fishermen. Still, it was hard to imagine how a puppy never before exposed to water could know how to swim. Upon our arrival, it was already dark. I illuminated the pier and floating dock with outdoor lights from the eave of the house. I walked there with Jackson in my arms, down the steps to the edge of the water. I can still remember how anxious I was. What if he sank and drowned? How would I ever explain it to Brooke? What would my friends think of me, the only person to ever buy a Labrador retriever that couldn't swim!

In the dark shadows there by the dock, I gently lowered him into the water and he instantly began to paddle around, his oversized feet the perfect motor. I was so proud, like a dad watching his son's first successful attempt at riding a bike.

I pulled him from the water and hugged his wet mass to my chest. This was the beginning of many adventures at the lake. This little piece of rural Alabama seemed to be Jackson's favorite place on earth. Whenever I planned to go to the lake, I had an old black backpack I would take to transport all my reading and writing material. When leaving for work, I carried a more appropriate and nicer leather bag. Jackson came to learn that anytime he saw me coming from my office with the backpack, I was headed for the lake. He would become excited and begin to dance and run for the front door. Once the door was opened, he would dash out to the truck, knowing full well which vehicle was the ride to the lake. On the rare occasion when he didn't get to go with me, as I drove away from the house, I would see him standing in front of the large window at the front of the house, stock still with a droopy mouth, disappointment etched in his expression. Yet when I returned, he would greet me at the door with a lick on the face. He held no grudges. This taught me the *lesson of forgiveness*.

The trip from our home in Vestavia Hills to our house on Lake Martin was 74 miles door to door. The trip itself was an adventure for Jackson. He rode in the back seat of the truck with his front legs propped on the console between the front seats. He would duck his head down, so he could see under the rearview mirror. Each time I drive my truck I am reminded of this pose of Jackson's. There are holes in the leather console caused by his paws and his weight when he stood there. I was so angry the day I discovered he had marred the truck's interior. Today they serve as a reminder of how much fun we had on those trips. My favorite fountain pen for writing is also dimpled with his teeth marks from when he was a puppy. He grabbed it when it fell from my desk, hid and chewed on it until I discovered him.

When not looking out the windshield from his perch on the console he would hang his head from the rear window, his large ears flapping. His cheeks pinned back by the wind made it look as if he were smiling.

The Dalai Lama once said, "There are only two days in the year when nothing can be done; one is called yesterday and the other is called tomorrow. So today is the right day to love, to believe and to mostly live." Jackson taught me that lesson well: *to live in the moment,* because it is the only one we are guaranteed.

Our lake house was about 20 feet above the lake's edge. A maze of interconnecting steps and decks connected the house to the dock on the water below. Jackson loved for me to stand on the upper deck and toss a tennis ball out into the water for his retrieval. When he was ready to play, he would find his tennis ball and bring it and drop it at your feet, then look up at you with those big, sad eyes as if to say, "Play with me. Please. Play with me." If you didn't pick it up he would grab it again and drop it at your feet, just to make sure you heard and saw it. Once I would throw it out into the lake he would charge down the decks and steps to the dock and then leap out into the water. He would find the ball, clutch it in his teeth and then swim slowly back to the dock, his tail gently swishing back and forth like a rudder. He would ascend the steps from the water and then run up top to repeat the fun. That run and swim to retrieve the ball took a lot of energy. We would endlessly play this game. Completely exhausted, he would continue the cycle as long as I would throw the ball. He was tireless, always focused on the task at hand. I often said I wished people were as focused on their task at work as Jackson was when he was playing ball. He taught me the *lesson of how a razor-like focus will overcome any obstacle.* When you picked the ball up, he would quiver in anticipation, never taking his eyes off the ball, frozen in contemplation. Once you tossed the ball, his bound-up energy would release in a fury of motion toward the lake where he knew he would find the ball. Jackson would play this game dozens of times on a hot summer's day.

One of my favorite pastimes at the lake, was sitting on the large deck beneath the canopy of trees, reading. The lake was eerily quiet. I often said we never know the noise pollution we have in the city, until we come to a place like this. There was a small fountain by the deck and the sound of the rippling water, the only sound to the quiet backdrop of the woods around me, always made for such a serene setting. While I read, Jackson would lie at my feet and observe the woods around us. He was like a little child, cocking his head at every new sound. We spent hours upon hours like this. Many a day I would have to chase him down after an errant turkey or deer would wander into our clearing and he would take off in hot pursuit. Jackson taught me the *lesson of companionship*, how to be still in the moment and enjoy the one you are with.

I worried about Jackson and snakes at the lake. He was so curious, he had to investigate every movement. Twice, I had to chase him away from a snake he found on the property, once down by the water, and another when I let him out to pee, one night under the floodlights out back. He was very protective of his territory there, not wanting other wild and furry things on his property. Once a flock of geese landed in the cove in front of our house. We watched from the screened porch as they swam toward our dock. All of a sudden there was a brown blur running across the deck and splashing into the water as Jackson charged their position. They scattered in many directions and I never saw a goose in our cove again. Then there was the time shortly after we moved into the cabin and were having breakfast on the porch. Jackson strolled up with his own breakfast, a freshly killed rabbit whose demise came as a result of trespassing on our property.

Back in Birmingham, Kathy taught Jackson to retrieve the newspaper from our front lawn each morning. He would wait by the door when we arose, waiting to do his duty. He knew he always got a treat for his labor. You had to make sure no one was walking a dog when you opened the door. Jackson loved to rush to greet neighborhood pets and their owners who might be walking by our house. He was completely harmless, but seeing the 90-pound mass of teeth and fur rushing at you did not appear harmless!

When he returned with the paper, he would drop it at your feet and wait for his treat, Bacon, the doggy bacon that comes in those bright yellow packages. It took a while for him to learn that ours was the only paper he was supposed to retrieve. He saw every paper up and down the street as redeemable for bacon at our house. There was a time when we went on vacation for a few days and a friend of our daughter stayed with Jackson. One morning she let him out to get the paper, and she returned a few minutes later to a pile of papers on our porch. She was concerned because she didn't know to whom they belonged.

B.J., our smaller dog, would always stand at the window and watch Jackson charge out into the cold and rain to do his job. When Jackson returned with the paper and expected his treat, B.J. would line up with him for his treat, though he did nothing to deserve it. I nicknamed B.J. "the welfare dog."

From these tasks Jackson taught me *the lesson of servanthood*. It mattered not the weather outside or how he felt; he performed his duty each morning without fail or procrastination.

One of the tragedies of this period of our lives was the loss of B.J., our peekapoo. While preparing for a spring break trip to Disney and loading the car late one spring night, B.J. slipped outside and was watching us load the car. She was older now, and her hearing was fading. She had wandered across the street in the dark. Kathy had called for her just as a neighbor's visitor was driving away across the street. B.J. stepped in front of the approaching car and died in my arms moments later. Hearing the commotion outside, Jackson ran out and eased up beside me. Dogs can sense death. He immediately ran back to the house, up the stairs and lay beneath our bed. Jackson would always get beneath the bed when he was scared or sad, usually when thunder raked the skies or fireworks were exploding on the holidays. For weeks on end after B.J.'s death, Jackson moped around the house, sadness clearly etched in his face. He missed his playmate.

John, Brooke's then-boyfriend and now her husband and the father of three of our grandchildren, loved to play Frisbee with Jackson. I have already mentioned that Jackson was a world-class athlete. He would chase after a soaring Frisbee, leap high in the air at precisely the right moment to catch it while it soared across our yard, then gracefully alight, and return it to John to repeat the feat. I would often look out the window to our front yard while Jackson was performing his agile catches to see a gaggle of neighborhood children watching in awe. I think John enjoyed this as much as Jackson did!

I have always heard how Labs are good with children. This became apparent as we started to accumulate grandchildren. Jackson was always so gentle around them and protective. He knew exactly whom he was dealing with during playtime. When I played tug-of-war with him, his jaws were like a vise. He clamped so hard it was impossible to get the object from him. But if it was one of the children playing with him, his clutch was much less vigorous. He playfully "bit" at me when I would take something from him, just hard enough to let me know he was not happy. He would never do that with the children. He would often lay in the floor and let the children crawl all over him without a whimper. It was obvious he loved children. The way he behaved around little children taught us *the lesson of gentleness and patience.*

In 2009, we moved to a new home. This house had a nice garden enclosed by a wall out back but did not have a "doggy door," like our previous house. This was a bit inconvenient for Jackson, as he now had to be let out when he needed to relieve himself. He soon learned to come to us and bark when he wanted to go outside.

The new house had a steep driveway. Jackson learned to retrieve our paper here, but within a year or so his aging was causing him to have difficulty getting up and down the hill. The vet had told us that Jackson had no cartilage between the bones in his knees. This had to be very painful for him. He could no longer take long walks with us or perform other kinds of exercise, which he needed.

In the fall of 2011, Jackson had an accident that hastened his physical decline. While we were away at a ball game in Tuscaloosa, Mike's caregiver let Jackson out into the garden for his normal business. In the garden was a heavy cement birdbath that Jackson loved to drink from. Somehow the birdbath had become unsteady on the soft soil of the flower garden. When Jackson reared up to put his front paws on the bowl of the birdbath it turned over, pinning him beneath its heavy weight. The caregiver was able to get the heavy bowl off him but he lay prone, unable to get up and walk. He simply pulled himself a few feet with his front legs and could not go further.

When we arrived home hours later, his condition remained the same. He would crawl with his front legs, pulling his motionless hind legs along behind him. I took him to an emergency animal clinic that evening. At the vet, they got him up and he hobbled about. The vet noticed something strange in his gait and said he had some spine involvement. He suggested maybe it was just bruised and inflamed from the accident, but they wanted to keep him overnight. I called the next morning to learn they had x-rayed him and there was no broken back, but he still would not stand. They asked us to come over that afternoon and we would make some decision as to a course of action. I fully expected to have to put him down. Brooke went with us that evening to see Jackson. Upon arrival, we were told there still was no change and we were led back to "dog ICU" to see him. He was lying still as a mouse in a cage with IV'S hooked to both legs. When he saw us, he jumped to his feet and began to lunge at the cage, trying to get to us. The vet was amazed. They unhooked him from the IV lines and got him out of the cage. He was so happy to see us, now standing on all fours. The doctor was amazed again. He said the only problem was that his kidneys weren't functioning. He hadn't urinated in 24 hours. They took him outside and he immediately peed. The doctor told us he was going to send him home with us. He also informed us that he had found a broken bone in Jackson's right rear leg and had put a cast on it but recommended we see our regular vet Monday. We left the vet with joy, knowing Jackson would be with us a while longer. Kathy slept that night on a mattress on the floor with him.

I took him to our vet on Monday. After taking more x-rays, the vet told me he didn't think Jackson's leg would heal because the bones were not together. He suggested doing surgery to pin the bone together. He even showed me x-rays of a dog he had done this to recently. We agreed. Jackson came through the surgery fine but had to wear a hard cast on his leg for about six weeks. At first, he wouldn't walk on the leg, so we had to make a belly band to slip around him to help him negotiate the two steps out into the garden and to transport him from his bed in the den to his bed in our bedroom. After a few weeks, he began to walk with the cast.

When the cast came off, he would not put weight on the leg. The vet told us eventually he would start to use it again, and he did.

It seemed Jackson was never the same physically after this accident. It was obvious he was growing old and weary. In February, I made a trip to Louisiana to attend Mardi Gras with friends who lived there. While I was away, Jackson made another escape. During the night, Kathy had let Jackson out in the garden to do his business. She fell asleep in a chair while she was waiting on him. When she woke in the early light of the new day and went out back, she found the gate had been left open and Jackson was nowhere to be found. It was a cold morning with ice from the drizzle the night before forming on the roads. Kathy began to walk the neighborhood and call for Jackson. Just beyond our house on the street out front, she heard a whimper from a ravine just a few yards off the road as she called Jackson's name. There was a small creek that ran there behind a neighbor's house. Upon investigation, she found Jackson down in the creek, his rear legs pinned between two large rocks. She struggled to free him. He was cold and shivering with ice forming on his nose. She finally got him out. She used her coat as a bellyband to help get him back to the house. At the vet, she was relieved to find there were no broken bones, but he had been exposed to the elements for a long time and was sick for several days.

Jackson's mobility continued to decline. He could not walk very far without plopping down on his hindquarters. We would sometimes have to help lift him into a standing position. His back legs would sometimes just slip out from under him, causing him to fall. It was hard for him to negotiate the two steps out of the house into the garden. He could go down the steps to our quarters in the basement but could not climb back up. He would have to be led around the house to the upper garage to re-enter our main level. It was so sad to watch. We knew we were being unfair to

Jackson to keep him with us in such pain.

One Wednesday in midsummer we discussed the inevitable and called the vet. They assured us we were doing the right thing and gave us an appointment for the next morning. This was one of the longest, saddest days of my life. Knowing the next day would be Jackson's last with us was agonizing. It was hard to look into his eyes. That night I cooked a huge steak and fed the entire thing to him. Kathy slept that night on the floor with him on a blanket beside his bed.

As we loaded him up the next morning, he seemed a bit excited as he always did when he got to go for a ride. I almost felt as if I was deceiving him. He did not know he would not return to his home and his family.

Kathy got in the cargo area and held him on the way to the vet. Once there, they put us in a private room with Jackson and explained what would happen. Jackson lay in the floor, his head in Kathy's lap. She hadn't left his side since the night before. They shaved his front leg and gave him an injection to make him sleep. Then they administered the drug that would stop his heart. He breathed a deep breath and lay still. Then he took another deep breath and was gone. The tears flowed as the vet told us to stay with him as long as we'd like. After a few minutes, we clipped some gray hairs from around his mouth and placed them in a baggie. We left him to be cremated. His ashes now sit atop our fireplace mantel in a box with a brass plate with his name inscribed. He so enjoyed lying there in front of a fire on a cold winter's day. He can now continue to watch over us, and we can feel close to him.

As I reflect on those final weeks with Jackson, when he always wanted to be close to us, I realize he was teaching me another lesson: *that this season of your life is not going to last forever.*

Good or bad, it will soon pass, never to be visited again. Relish the moment.

In the days since Jackson left us, we have fondly recalled his many misadventures and all the good times. We miss him terribly. When we eat dinner on trays in front of the TV, we're sad to remember how he would lie beneath them waiting on the errant morsel to fall to the floor, or barking at the breakfast table for his share. I still slide my feet when I walk through the house at night, so as not to step on him sleeping in one of the hallways. I suddenly sit up in bed, thinking he is nudging my arm to let me know he needs to go outside.

There is one thing we have all realized. We didn't choose the wrong puppy after all. He chose us on that chilly fall morning fourteen years ago. And he was the perfect dog for us.

RIP Jackson...*and thanks for all the lessons and love.*

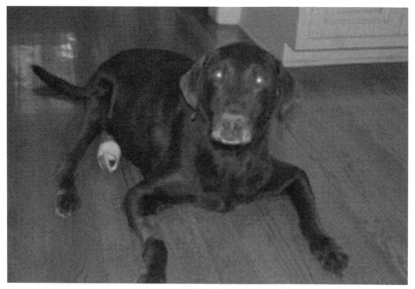

Jackson

7

Big Daddy

****

It has always seemed strange to me how our memory lays down tracks. Sometimes small unimportant things seem to scratch their way down into my memory while more noteworthy things don't register.

My grandfather, Howard M. Posey, died in 1958 at the National Jewish Hospital in Denver, Colorado. His doctors in Alabama recommended this hospital for treatment of his tuberculosis, as it was one of the leading lung hospitals in the country at the time. He died there of complications from surgery at 57 years of age.

The summer before his death, we drove to Denver to visit him. One morning, as we traveled through the West, we stopped for breakfast and buffalo was on the menu. I threw a tantrum to have that, but was denied. I am sure it was quite expensive and not within our budget.

We still have videos of that visit, of me playing in the snow in July up in the mountains, and us walking with Big Daddy in a garden on the hospital grounds.

My grandmother, Pearl Davis Posey, rented a room in the home of a lady who lived near the hospital while my grandfather was a patient there. I remember a large cherry tree in the yard of the boarding house. I had never seen such a tree and was impassioned by the sweet red fruit that was abundant in its branches. I gorged myself until I became sick.

My last memory of my grandfather is from that trip. He was gaunt. Surgery had left a huge scar that arced from the front of his chest, beneath his right arm and up his back. Seeing his family caused him to smile through his pain.

He died in September after our visit in July. I was 7 years old at the time. My mother was an only child and extremely close to her father. She was inconsolable that night. I can still remember her anguish for months on end after his death

My first memory of my grandfather is waking one morning to hear the excitement of my brother Mike and sister Kay as they discovered my grandfather entering the yard with a horse buggy he had bought for them. The buggy had a leather carriage top with a small window in the back. It was jet black except for the wooden wheels, shafts and seat, which were bright red. I can still hear the grinding metallic sound of the steel-rimmed wooden wheels as they traversed the alleys around town.

A horse named Lady pulled the buggy. There were many horses in the family in those days. I, being the youngest of three grandkids, only remember Lady. My brother and sister had a fondness for horses that guaranteed my grandfather would always see to it that they had one.

A tragedy, that happened before I was old enough to remember, scarred my brother. Before Lady, he had a horse he named Trigger, I'm sure it was eponymously named after Roy Rogers famous horse because he watched that television show every Saturday morning. Trigger was boarded in a small barn that sat next to the railroad tracks behind my grandparent's house. Beside the barn was a small fenced area where the horse could exercise. On the night of the tragedy, a plow blade with rows of sharp disc had been leaned against one side of the barn. A thunderstorm occurred late in the night and frightened the horse. Trigger would rear up on his hind legs when these storms came through and thrash about. When Mike came to check on the horse in the morning, he found him dead on the floor of the barn. Blood was everywhere. Evidently during Trigger's meltdown during the storm, he reared up and his neck came down on one of the plowing disc and severed major arteries.

At 6 years of age, I was my grandfather's side-kick. We would ride around town and the countryside near Piedmont in his 1950 model gray Plymouth. First stop on these excursions was always the grocery store on Ladiga Street. My grandfather had once owned the grocery, but I think at this time it was run by Carmey Davis. The purpose of the grocery stop was to grab a handful of peanut butter logs. You could get a double handful for 5 cents. These were semi-hard candies with a peanut butter filling. You can still buy them today, but they don't taste the same. My purchase would be placed in a small brown paper bag, which was then placed in the seat of the Plymouth for Big Daddy and me to share as we rode around town.

One memorable trip took us to the house of one of my grandfather's friends. He lived in a small pink house out on Highway 9 in the Nances Creek area. Upon arrival, he greeted us out by his strawberry patch. We gathered some of the fruit in one of those woven wooden baskets, then washed them with water from the well. We sat at a small wooden table in the kitchen and I ate the freshly picked berries covered with sugar and cream.

That old pink house stood for many years. I would pass it many times as a teenager and it always brought back fond memories.

One of my last vivid images of my grandfather at his home must be from the time just before my grandparents left for Denver. I would be playing in the yard and see him rocking on the front porch of his house next door. He would beckon me to his side and would reach in his pocket and bring forth a nickel and place it in my hand. "You are gonna save that now, aren't you?" "Yes sir, I'd reply."

I would then run as fast as my short legs would take me to the gas station on the northwest corner of Main and Smith Street, just a hundred yards or so from my grandfather's front porch. There I would drop my nickel in the Coke machine out front, pull the large rubber handle, and receive an ice-cold Coca-Cola, the bottle sweating in the summer heat. All this took place in full view of my grandfather on the porch, laughing as I broke my promise to him of saving that nickel. That scene repeated itself many times during my early years.

Big Daddy was only fifty seven when he died. He seemed old then. Fifty-seven now seems so young, at least for death.

My grandfather always kept a whiskey bottle hidden in a warehouse out behind his grocery store. He would often sneak out back at the end of a day's work and share a swig with the hired help. My grandmother always believed that is how he contracted the tuberculosis.

Mommie Pearl and Big Daddy owned several businesses. When Mother was small they owned the Little Gem Café. It sat beside the train station on Center Avenue. Mommie Pearl would make sandwiches there and peddle them to the fares on the train when it would stop at the depot next door. That restaurant was still there when I was a teenager, then owned by the Payne family.

In addition to the restaurant and grocery business, my grandfather would buy and sell land, build and sell houses and farm cotton.

He must have been a fair businessman, but a bit too kindhearted. After my grandmother died, I found a large container of cigar boxes filled with unpaid credit bills people had charged at the grocery and never paid. I've been told that when times were hard, she would go door to door with those cigar boxes under her arm trying to collect. Big Daddy was too benevolent to do that, I am told. He would never lean on a man who owed him money if the man was going through hard times.

That old '50 Plymouth later became my first car when I began to drive. It was as large as a living room inside. Gray felt like cloth covered the seats, and the dashboard was made of metal. A large silver knob on the dash operated the one speed windshield wipers. I remember handgrenading the engine coming down Fifth Avenue, by Lawtex, one late summer day. We never repaired the car after that. Its time was finished. Two cars later marked the finish of my carefree days in Piedmont. I would soon leave for college and then a family and career...but, oh what a heart full of memories I left with.

Today, when I give my grandchildren a dollar, I flash back to my time with Big Daddy, and unconsciously say "You are gonna save that now, aren't you?"

8

Swimming Holes

****

Seems every child that grew up in rural America had a favorite swimming hole. Lakes don't count because most are man-made. Swimming holes are made by God-- nestled in the woods, flowing through valleys and pastures, often only accessible from a weedy path, or by climbing under a wooden bridge that crossed its girth.

Children around Piedmont were blessed with plenty of natural streams that meandered through the countryside, their serpentine paths forming pools along the way in which to while away a hot summer's day.

The first one I remember was Neighbors' swimming hole, eponymously named for a family that once owned the farm it coursed through. Some summer days would find friends and me there on our bikes without swim trunks. No matter. We'd park our bikes by the bridge on a narrow dirt road, crawl through a barbed wire fence, and walk the short distance across the pasture to the water's edge, all the while dodging cow patties abundantly scattered around the field. There, beneath a giant spreading oak tree, we would do what came natural to us: shed our clothes.

One thing all these streams had in common was that they were all numbingly cold. One particular day spent at Neighbors' swimming hole is painfully etched in my memory. While we were in the creek that day, we were surprised by the arrival of two girls with their mother, come to refresh themselves in the stream. Of course, we boys were sans swim trunks.

The water there was often the color of creamed coffee because of the Alabama red clay that formed the streambed. We were protected from being discovered naked as long as we stayed in the water, just our heads above the surface. Normally we would get out of the water every ten minutes or so to get our struggling circulation back up. After twenty minutes or so we would return to the creek. Obviously, this was not possible that day. We were held hostage by our nakedness!

The girls would jump in the water, quickly climb out, then sun themselves on towels at the edge of the stream. It seemed they would never leave! When they finally did, we dragged our purple, shriveled bodies from the ice bath and laid in all our nakedness beneath the August sun, shaking like old women with palsy. One of my friends shared one of his Swisher Sweets cigarillos – my first taste of sin. Eventually we dressed and waddled to our bikes, vowing to never swim here again without proper attire.

Another favorite place to swim was called "Second Bridge". There were three bridges that spanned Terrapin Creek out east of town. The second of these three bridges provided a great place to swim. My dad would take us there on Sunday afternoons; it was too far to ride a bike. We would park on the narrow shoulder of the road and scurry down a steep path by the bridge. A natural beach had formed there by the water's edge from years of alluvial deposits.

It was such a picturesque place. The water flowed over rocks under the bridge forming a rapid, then slowed and pooled, forming a deep swimming hole whose rock bottom gradually shallowed next to the sandy shore. I remember the clean, fresh smell that always emanated from the stream, the mist formed by the cold-water cascading over the rocks in the warm summer air, the verdant creek bank that smelled of sweet wildflowers and rhododendron. The emerald green water always left you feeling clean, unlike the cloying chlorine water in the public pools in town.

I once found a perfectly formed fossil of a fish about six inches long embedded in a flat rock I brought up from the creek's bottom. I graciously gave it up to a science teacher at school for use in her class.

Forty Foot was another place to swim, not far from Second Bridge. You could drive your car right to the creek bank. Train tracks ran along a hillside on the far side of the creek. Legend had it that a train once derailed here and plunged into the creek, never to be retrieved from its depths. Teens would tell younger kids that when they grew older they would be able to hold their breath long enough and dive deep enough to see the skeleton of the rusty train.

Another popular swimming hole was a place called Crouches Island, north of town off Highway 9, also on Terrapin Creek. Crouches Island was also a great place to camp. As a result, it got lots of visitors.

Somewhere along its rocky bottom lies a gold ring with a March birthstone. It was given to me by my girlfriend, and future wife, and lost that summer of '68 while I swam.

As a child, I often fished way upstream from Crouches at a cabin in the curve off Highway 9 called the Fred Roberts Place. I assumed Mr. Roberts had once been the owner of the cabin. I sat on a large rock and fished. I once went there with a brand-new fishing rod and reel and lost it almost immediately when I carelessly laid it by my side and a gar took the line and dragged the rod into the creek. Never did find that rod. It had taken near a week's salary of mowing lawns beneath the hot Alabama sun to purchase it, and it was gone in a flash. A small price to pay, I guess, for the solitude and blessing of spending time in such a beautiful place.

In the early '90s' I'd go back near Crouches Island with my father to a place called Seven Springs. There beside the creek; clear, cold water bubbled up from the depths of the earth, purified on its journey through the labyrinth of limestone it passed on its way to the surface. We'd take gallon milk jugs and fill them with the spring water. It made everything taste better. I've drunk lots of spring water since, much of it exceptional, but none quite as good as the cool water that bubbled up from Seven Springs.

One day we arrived to fetch water and were greeted by a fence across the path that led down to the spring. A sign attached to the fence post read "No Trespassing." Some scoundrel had probably littered the property with beer bottles or otherwise defaced the land. Can't blame the owners.

Years later I discovered another stream in the county near Jacksonville. Actually, I was taken there by a friend. We drove down a narrow, rutted lane in my Jeep, then drove along an overgrown field through a copse of trees to the stream. My cousin took his tractor there and carved out a ramp so we could enter in my Jeep. The rock bottom and shallow water allowed me to drive into the creek, go about fifty yards upstream and park where the creek bottom dropped off into a deeper pool fed by a small waterfall. The temperature always seemed to drop five or ten degrees once you entered the stream and parked beneath the canopy formed by the large trees that shaded it.

There I spent many summer afternoons. I would take a chair and small table and sit them in the stream behind my Jeep. I spent countless hours there reading and writing. As more people discovered the little oasis, more came. I noticed litter along its bank and would find bottles on the creek bottom. Trails were cut in the surrounding woods by four-wheelers. The silence, once only broken by the gurgling stream and gentle waterfall, was now shattered by carousing teenager's loud music and profanity. Then one day I arrived at the end of the lane to find a gate had been erected to block the entrance, and the dreaded "No Trespassing" sign hung from it.

On the drive back home I was struck by the thought of how often our privileges are taken away because others abuse the privilege; others lack respect for the land. Mostly I've come to realize that we don't truly value simple things until they are taken away from us. Swimming holes and the fragrant hinterlands of Piedmont nurtured me in my youth. They still do today.

Swimming Holes

Second Bridge

9

Piled Upon One Another

****

Thomas Jefferson once said, "When we get piled upon one another in large cities, as in Europe, we shall become as corrupt as Europe."

I think we have arrived at the destination Jefferson warned us about. Worst of all we are becoming so calloused that we hardly notice it; at least we pay little mind to it. That is, until something reminds us of how it used to be.

This Friday past I attended a funeral in my hometown of Piedmont, Alabama. This small hamlet lies where the Appalachian mountain range begins, the foothills of Northeast Alabama.

There are few sites in Alabama more picturesque than looking down on Piedmont from Highland Cemetery, the town below nestled up against the lush hills surrounding it at the base of Dugger Mountain.

Arriving early, I drove to the cemetery to visit the graves of several ancestors laid to rest there, the most recent that of my late father. I sat on a bench taking in the beauty and solitude of the town spread out below, a place unadulterated by the raucousness of a city.

Later, after the funeral at Thompson Funeral Home, a local police car led the funeral procession as it snaked along the route to Memory Gardens, where the loved one would be interred.

As the procession moved along, I noticed oncoming traffic pulling to the side. I even saw a walker who stopped and stood in reverence as we passed. Every single car along the route paused. Wherever they were going, whatever pressing thing they had to do, could wait for the few minutes it would take for the deceased to pass. It is just what you do in this town. It is a matter of respect for your neighbor. I've noticed that in the city, people have long since lost this courtesy, this reverence and respect for their neighbor. They are far too busy to stop for a dead man, even for a minute.

As we approached the entrance to the cemetery, the policeman parked his cruiser so as to stop oncoming traffic. He then climbed from the car, removed his hat, and stood at attention as we entered the cemetery. You wouldn't see that in the big city, not for an ordinary citizen. I guess we've become to "Piled upon one another."

I remembered another day more than 20 years ago when I had moved my family to South Florida for a promotion at work. We lived in the Miami/Ft. Lauderdale area for three years.

At the first PTA meeting, we were greeted by teachers who were so impressed that our son was so polite, that he always addressed them with "yes ma'am" and "yes sir." We were shocked to find that a child showing respect for his teachers was an occasion for recognition. This was the same reason we moved back to the "real South" at the first opportunity.

The last Christmas we were in South Florida, we drove back to Piedmont to spend the holidays with family. We made the 12-hour trip during the night so the children were asleep. As we eased into Piedmont in the early morning light, out of the corner of my eye, I saw an elderly walker make a motion from the sidewalk as we passed. I looked at my wife and said "Did he just flip me off?" She laughed and said "You have been away from the South too long; he was just waving to us."

You see, in Miami, the only place in the South where they say you go south to go north, one would never wave a good morning greeting, especially to a complete stranger. Most of the residents of South Florida are transplants from the North who were "piled upon one another."

One of the major reasons we moved back to Alabama was, so our children could learn the grace and charm and good manners that are handed down here from one generation to the next like a family heirloom.

I'm not suggesting that the South has cornered the market on manners and kindness and respect for your neighbor. But it sure seems that way when you've been away for a while and return to Piedmont, Alabama.

10

Den of Sin

****

This is for the guys: the few who risked their reputations, risked losing all comport with the community and forevermore be considered living in total debauchery! For all this was considered to be your lot in life should you choose to enter that sordid establishment on North Center Avenue known simply as "The Pool Room."

To my recollection, there was no neon sign that called it such, just an indiscreet narrow placard that hung from its demonic facade that read, *Billiards,* a name usually reserved for more gentlemanly establishments. We were told from the time we were old enough for Sunday school we should not go near the place. Some children were so frightened of the building that they would cross the street to avoid walking in front of its swinging doors, lest some foul something was to lunge from its dark interior and sweep them inside.

I must have been about fifteen when I finally screwed up the courage to march in, and then only from the rear entrance in the back alley. God forbid that someone see me and tell my parents. I never considered that my uncle, who owned the place and was omnipresent, to be a risk factor. I truly expected to become apoplectic the first time I entered the unseemly place. I justified my early presence there through my Sunday school lessons, should someone see me. I would tell them that Jesus ate and drank with sinners. "Look it up, it's in your Bible." Through my piety, these miscreants might come to know the Lord. I was much like Paul, willing to risk it all. Those thoughts always made me feel better.

The inside of the pool hall was always dimly lit, except for the long, low lights that hung over the billiard tables. Each light was controlled by a string that you pulled to turn it on when you played and turn it off when you were finished. Customers always did this out of habit. If a light over a table was on, it was being used; if it was dark, it was available.

Sometimes it was busy, and you had to wait for a table. There was no list to put your name on like in these overpriced restaurants now, or a number to take like at my local bakery. It was gentleman's etiquette. You simply observed who was waiting when you came in and you took your turn when it was time. We did the same thing at the barber shop.

There was always a cloud of smoke that hung over the place, like some miasma, emanating from mostly unfiltered Camels and Pall Malls. The billiard tables were a thing of beauty, unlike the amateur things you see in stores today. These tables were for real men. They were made of heavy, burly wood, smoothed by steady hands over the years, pockmarked with cigarette burns where some errant player had laid his smoke while he contemplated a shot. The felt was green and faded from years of use, but the heavy slate table beneath was as true as a surgeon's hand. The pockets were of braided leather. Even today I can close my eyes and hear the crack of the rack as someone breaks a game of nine ball and hear the swoosh as the balls fall into the soft leather pockets. "Rack 'em Red."

Red Smith was the attendant and would rack them tight, dropping your 10-cent payment into the coin apron he wore around his waist. The cue sticks were held in racks along the walls. I shot an 18-ounce cue, still remember to this day. Once you selected your cue, you would roll it across the table to ensure that it was arrow straight. Little blue cubes of chalk lay along the rail of the table to coat the leather tips of the cues, thus ensuring grip on contact with the cue ball. You'd be hard- pressed to find a leather tip on a cue today, outside a fine establishment like that one.

Cans of talc were attached to the wall. You'd tap some in your palm and slide it along the cue, slick as a baby's butt, now you were ready to break.

The restroom was detached from the main building. You had to exit to the alley to enter the restroom. There was no men's or women's, just one. It didn't even have a door! No need. No self-respecting woman would dare walk down that alley, knowing the ever-present danger that would bring.

The county was dry at the time. But most anything you wanted could be had at the bootlegger's just south of town on Highway 9. It wasn't allowed in the poolroom. I had been told that at one time there was a bar where you could sit and order food. A man named Hilburn made chili that was served there. Hilburn's famous chili is still talked about with reverence around those parts. During my time, there was only a glass case with candy, snacks and cigarettes. There was of course a Coke machine. I had seen "The Hustler" with Paul Newman. This place was nothing like the places he plied his trade.

Small stakes gambling would take place, though you rarely saw money change hands, as this was forbidden by local law and loosely enforced by the staff. The keno board was a wooden thing that could be placed at the end of a table, covering about a fourth of the table's area. The front of the board had a ramp to allow balls to roll up. To begin the game, players would select a pill from a leather bottle issued by the attendant. The object was to land a ball in the numbered hole you drew. Your number was kept secretly in your pocket. If an opponent landed a ball in your hole, you won. Anytime you saw the Keno board come out, you knew some serious betting was going on.

Occasionally a stranger from out of town would come in carrying a custom- made cue in a leather case. A custom-made cue was a badge that claimed you had reached a certain skill level. These players would shoot a round or two with a companion or local, carefully disguising their skill level until challenged by someone who didn't know the game they played. Thus, came the term "hustler." A good player would lure you in by playing below his capability, lose a few, and then start raising your bet. Obviously, these people were frowned upon, or worse.

Before I became proficient and could compete in these games myself, I would study the good players. There were seats along the wall, up on platforms, so you could see all the action. Up on those creaking wooden pedestals, ensconced in a chair not unlike those in the theater down the street, I learned about "english," the ability to rotate the cue ball for the next shot, how to use the table markers for bank shots and always playing a shot or two ahead. I also learned the "head games" people would play, which served me well later on.

Arnold Woolf, the proprietor, sat at a desk just inside the front entrance and to the left of its swinging doors. He would sit for hours under a dim yellow light from a desk lamp studying horse racing forms. I later learned that Arnold would travel to mysterious locations in New York, Florida, California and Kentucky where he would "play the ponies." I surmised later that Arnold was as close as I would ever come to a professional gambler. He did it at places where it was legal, and he did it with proficiency. There were parlays too, those small cards where the next week's football games were parsed. You could bet on multiple teams. A stranger from out of town would pick up the cards on Fridays. I guess the money would be delivered to the winners the same way the next week. I never played those parlays. I didn't know how to ask. It was a very secret ritual.

Years later, when Greentrack opened, an older friend of mine asked Arnold to take him there and teach him how to bet on the greyhounds. That first trip with Arnold, he was so proud; he took $50 and came back with over $350. My friend went back three more times to my knowledge, unfortunately without Arnold to tutor him. These trips were so costly to him that he quickly gave up the vice.

Several years before my Aunt Evelyn (Arnold's wife) passed away, I was visiting her one weekend in Piedmont. She asked me to be the executor of her will. We lived in Miami at the time, and I often drove by the famous horse track in Hialeah. I had mentioned this to my aunt, and she shared with me a small notebook Arnold had written with cryptic notes on how to bet the horses. There was instruction on what to look for physically, mudders, how to translate a racing form, and other interesting things, but again, all cryptically written so they were hard to decipher. She said Arnold had always planned on writing a book on the subject. She gave me the notebook, and I still have it in a safe deposit box. I never tried to use its wisdom.

A few years later, on another visit to Evelyn's, she told me that two men, nicely dressed in fine suits, had recently knocked at her door and introduced themselves as friends of her departed husband. They mentioned the notebook and wanted to purchase it. She explained that it had been given away. I'm glad she didn't say to whom. Sounds like they may have been from the south side of Chicago.

There were many characters I met at the pool hall over the years. I haven't mentioned names for obvious reasons. Those of you who frequented the place would know who they were by their nicknames, like Flopsy and Eight-Ball. After I moved away from Piedmont, I subscribed to the Piedmont Journal. Over the years, I watched many of those colorful men pass away through the obituaries in the paper.

I'm not sure when the pool room closed its doors for good. I have often wondered why it had such a dire reputation. Cursing and gambling went on there, but I could experience that at other places around town. I did learn some valuable life lessons there and whiled away many a happy day in its cool darkness.

I guess the last time I was in the pool hall was in the early '70s. I was a young adult then, out on my own. But I still entered the place through the alleyway, to avoid some pillar of the community seeing me and having my reputation cast into that filthy pit with the other dregs of society.

I have visited pool halls since, but always come away disappointed. They just don't measure up: no character and pomp like the one in my memory. It's best, I guess. I want to remember it like it was in the day, like so many other things from that era.

Pool Room

11

Ode to a Flea Market

They're not here to make a buck

Although they might with a little luck.

The thrill is the chase,

A bargain bought

Varied things here are sought.

Dishes, glass, an old iron bed,

Rusted items from Grandpa's shed.

Jewelry, books and antique clocks

Cloth, cloaks and bundles of socks.

A painted Indian with a broken arm,

Plastic livestock in an old red barn.

Hawking doughnuts, two bucks a throw

Cokes and fries and grape flavored snow.

Tim H. Webb

Redneck men with overweight wives

Barter with con men for three-dollar knives

Junk and treasure can both be found here

Items somebody once held dear.

What-cha take?

How much will you spend?

They dicker over tarnished and chipped bookends.

A stuffed red rooster and some broken earmuffs

It's hard to believe people buy this stuff!

A few pretty women and a lot of big butts

Cowboys and farmers and beer belly guts.

Old-timey people and items forlorned

It's the Collinsville flea market, Saturday morn.

12

Haunting Memories

****

From my birth until I was nine years old, we lived in a duplex apartment owned by my grandparents on Smith Street, also known as the Anniston Highway. The house sat next to my grandparents' home in Piedmont, Alabama. Our family lived in the right-side apartment, and various others rented the other side. The apartment consisted of a tight kitchen and living room, a small bath and my parents' bedroom on the first floor. A steep staircase led to two bedrooms upstairs – one for my sister, Kay, and the other shared by my brother, Mike, and me. The entire family shared the bath on the first floor.

I can still hear the loud hum of the large window fan that drew the heat from our bedroom upstairs on a hot summer's night.

The house stood hard beside the Seaboard Railroad, which bordered the small yard in back. The railroad and its surroundings provided endless entertainment in a time before electronic devices and smart phones. One of our primary forms of entertainment was seeing who could walk the rails the farthest without falling off.

A railroad trestle spanned a small creek to the west, beneath which we spent many a hot summer afternoon frolicking in the wet weather branch. The stream ran dry if we went without rain for a few weeks. Oil often floated atop the water in the ditch after a heavy rain. Workers at the Texaco station on the corner of Anniston Avenue and Smith Street probably dumped used motor oil in some drain that found its way to the ditch beneath the trestle. This was in the days before the Environmental Protection Agency.

The thick privet along the stream's banks served as our jungle when we played World War II soldiers and reenacted the war. We played all decked out in our army surplus from a store in Anniston: helmets, canteens and backpacks. Nothing was quite as exciting as a visit to that store. Many of the items we found there still had the soldiers' names stenciled on them. The store itself smelled old and musty, much like the army barracks from which their merchandise came.

I was so into the role of "army man" that I once told the barber at Buster's Barbershop that I wanted a GI haircut, not having a clue as to what it looked like, only that it was what "army men" had. You can imagine my surprise when the barber finished and spun me around to look in the mirror. I was bald and my ears stood out like a mule's!

I could throw away the butch wax! I was so mortified I wore my army helmet everywhere I went until my hair grew out. I only removed it to bathe and sleep. My embarrassment was nothing compared to my mother's fury when she saw me. Thank God, she didn't take me along when she stormed to the barbershop to give the barber an earful. Poor Mr. Martin! It wasn't his fault. He only did what his seven-year-old customer requested.

From that day forward, when I went for a haircut, I had to present a note from my mother with instructions on how my hair was to be cut.

The Bennett-Knight Furniture store a few blocks away was the source of large appliance boxes we converted into dwellings for camping out. We found the boxes late in the day behind the furniture store and dragged them through an alleyway, across the railroad tracks to the backyard, where we would carefully cut windows in the sides and make an entrance with a door, all cutouts of cardboard.

Next to my grandmother's house was a funeral home, the Mickelson Brown Mortuary. In those days, the proprietor was Oscar Mickelson. I remember my grandmother looking out her bedroom window at night and exclaiming, "someone has died – the embalming room light is on."

At night when I pray, I still ask for forgiveness for an incident that occurred one night when I was a young kid.

The large doors on the garage bay of the funeral home next door to my grandmother's house, where the hearse was parked, were left open at night. Inside the bay was a stack of Coca-Cola cases filled with returnable bottles of Coke, I presume to restock the refrigerator inside the building.

One night while camping out in the backyard in one of those boxes, my older brother made me a dare. Next thing I remember is stealthily crossing the yard and entering the dark garage bay of the funeral home, and in the shadows formed by a streetlight outside, I pilfered a couple of those warm Cokes. Back in the cardboard tent, we knocked holes in the caps of the purloined sodas with a scout knife, and drank the warm liquid from inside. I assume notorious outlaws began their careers of plunder in similar ways. These raids continued throughout the summer, until finally one night the Cokes were no longer there Fortunately for me, they simply moved them inside instead of setting some sort of booby trap to corral the thief. I'm sure they probably knew it was the miscreants next door who took their soda.

Sometimes on those forays to the furniture store to get the boxes, we stopped in at the bus depot next door that shared a building with a launderette. Mrs. Lindsey ran the bus station from a small sectioned-off part of the building near the front. Here she sold all manner of candy and drinks. For several years, a Dolly Madison Bakery store stood on the other side of the furniture store. I loved the small boat-shaped cakes they sold there. They were drenched in vanilla icing and topped with two halves of a pecan. In junior high school, we boys would often walk to the bus depot, or the bakery, to buy our lunch. So nutritious! Once we were old enough to drive, we would use our lunch hour to drive to the Dari King. My staples there were BBQ Fritos and Cherry Coke.

When I entered 3rd grade, we moved to a new home my parents built about four blocks south on Montview Road. I now lived across the alley from my third-grade teacher, Mrs. Paula Turk. Ever notice how you remember the name of every grammar school teacher you ever had? West, Street, Turk, Scroggins, Hulsey, Roberts. There. Those were my first- through sixth-grade teachers.

Mrs. Turk was much too convenient now. I had to study penmanship under her tutelage many afternoons after school. Those who see my handwriting today know that she was a miserable failure in teaching me how to neatly pen a letter, or was it me who failed? Thank goodness for computers and word processors.

I have vivid memories of terrible earaches I suffered that year at school. Mrs. Turk folded a towel and placed it atop the noisy radiators that heated our room and have me lay my head on the towel.

At my new home on Montview Road our camping continued, but now we were elevated in our abodes from cardboard boxes to tents, not store-bought but homemade, of course. We would tie a piece of rope around a tree in the backyard then run it to another tree and tie it, forming a line over which we would hang a blanket, stretch its sides out to form the tent and then anchor the edges with bricks. We used clothespins and towels to close the ends. A blanket was laid on the ground inside to form a floor.

I remember an old rusted metal lantern from our basement that was rescued to provide light in the tent at night. I can still smell the acrid fumes of the kerosene that was used to fuel it. I remember that blanket that formed the tent glowing from the lantern light inside. From the outside, you could see the cactus and totem poles that were stitched into the blanket illuminated by the lantern. I think we bought that blanket in a souvenir shop on some lonely Indian reservation in Arizona on a trip out west.

We got very little sleep on those nights we "camped out." In the wee hours of the morning we slipped from the tent to roam the streets of our neighborhood, just to see if we could do it without getting caught. Nothing mischievous, mind you. It just seemed daring to wander around the town when everyone was asleep.

I often awoke the next morning with chigger bites in the most painful places. My mom painted them with clear nail polish. The theory was that this would suffocate the tiny insects and relieve the itch after a while. I recently Googled that remedy on my computer to find it does not work. I already knew that. Even without Google, I told my mother that all those years ago, as I was in agony for days with no relief from her potion.

Later, when we got driver's licenses, our late nights expanded to more daring fare. One of my favorites was taking newbies, not yet exposed to the freedom an automobile could give you, to the Barlow house late at night. This had once been a grand old home of a prominent family, now long abandoned. It was haunted, we explained to the kids younger than us, who were at our mercy. We told of the evil spirits that had taken up residence there as we drove to the hilltop where it stood. We parked and watched for a candle to appear and then move from window to window, carried by a spirit now condemned to haunt the place. These excursions always worked best on a stormy night.

In the late summer of 1958, I awoke in my upstairs bedroom in the duplex to shrill screams from my parents' downstairs bedroom. I was only 7 years old and I thought my mother was being murdered. I leapt from bed and bounded down the stairs. There I found my father holding my mother tightly as they sat on the edge of the bed in the dim light of a bedside lamp. She was convulsed in agony from a pain far greater than that caused by physical insult. Hers was a deep blow to the soul, hysterics wrenching her body. A phone call had just informed my mom that her dad had passed away in a hospital in Denver, Colorado.

We had been to Denver the summer before to visit my grandparents. It was such a thrill when we went up in the mountains there in July and played in the scraps of snow that were still hanging on in the high altitude. Playing in the snow in the morning and going for a swim in the motel pool in the afternoon was unheard of for a kid from the deep South.

There was a young Greek man who was being treated at the hospital where my grandfather was a patient. Somehow, I still remember his name: Mike Macrakis. He was a budding artist and painted a portrait of my sister while we were there. A few years ago, when my aging parents had to be moved closer to us, I found that painting in a closet as we were cleaning out the house.

Several years before my mom passed away, she found a bundle of letters that my grandmother had written to the family during the time they were in Denver. My grandmother wrote of her daily activities, things that seemed trivial to her, but were a window for me into her life at a time I was too young to know. She wrote of being in a five and dime in November that was serving a Thanksgiving meal at the lunch counter for forty-nine cents. Money was tight, and she loved to find bargains like this. Many of her letters were written with a pencil. I noticed several letters written in ink. She said she was glad to be able to write with a pen since she found ink pens on sale in that same five and dime.

At Christmas a few years ago, mother gave me that bundle of letters wrapped in a gold ribbon. I don't think she knew, but it was one of the most precious gifts I ever received. Those letters were the genesis of my journaling. I began to keep a journal so that my children and grandchildren could peek back into my life, sometime far in the future. Hopefully they will be as entertained and educated by my journals as I was with those letters from my grandmother. Those letters and others I found that my dad had written my mom from his ship in the Pacific during World War II are some of my most prized possessions.

My dad flew to Denver to accompany my grandfather's body back to Piedmont. His body lay in state in the living room of his home. That was quite common in that day. A couple of men would "sit up" with the body during the night. My sister was a teenager at the time and dearly loved our grandfather. I vividly remember her hanging on the side of the casket for hours on end, tears streaming down her face.

My grandfather had many black acquaintances in town. I think he must have employed some of them from time to time. A group of black men arrived at the house one night when my grandfather was lying in state. This was 1958, a very different time. They didn't come to the front door but came to the back and knocked on the screen door. They ask my grandmother if it would be okay for them to come back to pay their respects when everyone had left. My grandmother ushered them right in. Even at that young age, I knew we were segregated from the blacks in town, though I didn't yet know the word for it. Even though folks kept to their own, I knew there was respect among those folks and my grandparents. Later my grandmother called those same men over and gave them all my grandfather's clothes.

Race relations are different now. They have gotten better; they need to get better yet. As I watched the recent race riots in Ferguson, Missouri, I thought back to the time when my grandfather died. I've said many times that it is an embarrassment for me now to remember how Coloreds, as they were called then, were discriminated against in those days. I remember trips to the Sears store in Anniston and seeing two different water fountains on the wall, one marked "Colored," the other marked "White." I watched the news on our black and white Philco TV from Greensboro, North Carolina, when Coloreds formed a sit-in at a lunch counter at Woolworth's Five and Dime that only allowed Whites. I don't know, but even with the discrimination, it seems to me, there was more respect among the races then, at least among small town folk.

Still, as ashamed as I am of those days, I know, as Denys Winstanley once said, "...nothing is more unfair than to judge the men of the past by the ideas of the present." Still, there is no defense for how blacks were treated in those days. I am one of a generation that may be the first in the South to be embarrassed by segregation and have tried to embrace people of all races, but there is still much angst on both sides of the issue, though those of us living today had nothing to do with the matter on either side.

My grandfather was fifty-seven years of age when he passed. I saw my fifty- seventh birthday years ago. Fifty-seven seemed old to a seven-year-old. Not so much anymore. After his death, my grandmother was very lonely. She did whatever she could to make a little money to supplement her savings. She crocheted and quilted. A few years ago, Kathy and I decided to give afghans Mommie Pearl had made, to our children as an extra little gift at Christmas. Each one contained a letter from me about the love their great-grandmother had for her family. She would be so proud to know that we still use her afghans to keep us warm on chilly nights.

All those houses from my childhood still stand. My grandmother's, the duplex next door where we lived when my grandfather died, the house on Montview Road, and even the house Mrs. Turk lived in across the alley.

All of those who occupied the houses are gone. New residents write their own chapters now. My mom rented the properties for years after we moved my parents to Birmingham. It became too much. I would often have to drive her there to try and collect rent that was months in arrears. Expensive repairs had to be negotiated from afar. Just before her death, we sold all the properties in Piedmont, our last roots in a place where I grew up. Truth is, that place no longer exists. Oh, there are still good people there. But most of the industries that employed folks back then are gone, like Lawtex and Standard Coosa-Thatcher. Where once there were new Ford, Chevy, Oldsmobile and Pontiac car dealerships, empty buildings stand in disrepair.

Some say that meth labs have replaced the bootleggers. Most of the mom-and-pop groceries, precursors to modern day 7-

Elevens, are gone. There used to be so many. Candy was still a nickel at Chaffin's down Smith Street near the hospital and at Hart's out on the old Gadsden Highway, before the bypass was built. Garmany's across from the radio station and Purcell's where the Farmers & Merchants Bank now stands were convenient. H.J. Morgan's on Center Avenue, L.H. Howell's down near the village, and the old M and T Market across from the Mill are all long past. But I still have my memories. I still remember buying my sweetheart, whom I have now been happily married to for forty-six years, the largest box of Valentine candy available at Watson Drugs. I remember sodas at the old Meadow's Drug Store where, as a teen, I watched as a man swallowed an Alka-Seltzer tablet then drank a Coke after it. The old man erupted like Mount Vesuvius, but there was no rescue squad in those days.

There were visits to Dr. York's dental office between the Kwik Chek and Bennett's Ford and later to Dr. Reid over by Purdy's Drugs.

Memories, like driving through town on a Friday night from the Dari King to Frady's Coffee Cup and back again, turning the corner at Bud Kirk's Pure Oil station on the corner of Center Avenue and Ladiga Street, where the city gazebo now stands. We'd stop by the Y to see who was skating and maybe hook up. We attended football games at the old Victory Field and played in the vines that grew behind the Visitors' bleachers there. Gert and Bert, remember those concession stand days?

Things rot and rust and die off. People pass and move away. But memories? Memories are permanent, at least as long as we are sane. I guess that's why I like to travel so. I don't buy souvenirs very often. The memories are enough. More than enough. Memories are the only things no one can take away from us. Old age sometimes does, like that song about an aging old man looking in the mirror and saying, "It Ain't Me."

Fact of the matter is that those memories, living them, is what causes us to age: remembrance of old times, old friends and gone-away places recorded in every wrinkle, like the tracks on a phonograph record. We can play them back whenever we want, and it costs nothing. That's why memories are priceless. We who have lived long enough to have them are privileged.

In an outdoor space in our garden, by a fireplace we recently built, I have an old clay tablet standing in an easel that reads:

"Old wood to burn

Old wine to drink

Old friends to trust

Old books to read"

Those are the things that bring me happiness today.

Bennett-Knight Furniture and the Bus Depot

13

WPID

****

At the age of fifteen, I became an accidental disc jockey. My brother Mike, the one who had trained to be one, let me hang out with him at the local radio station. He taught me all there was to know: how to cue a record or load a cart for a commercial; how to take readings from the large transformers that formed one entire wall of the studio; how to turn on and off the broadcast equipment, its tubes so ancient and petulant as to require nurturing to come to life on a cold winter's morning. By this time, I had learned to do every job at the station, from gathering the news from the loud UPI teletype machine in the lobby to cataloging records, sweeping the floor, taking out the trash-everything except speaking over the air.

Then came that fateful Sunday morning when my brother's car was found overturned in a creek off a highway near Jacksonville, Alabama. The car was obscured from the road by the dense overgrowth on the banks of the stream. It was daylight by the time a passing motorist saw a wheel of the car just visible from the bridge railings.

My brother survived, but had a severely broken leg, the one that was not affected by the polio he had suffered as a child. He had someone call me from the hospital when he arrived there by ambulance and instructed me to sign on the station that morning. I don't remember if it was cleared by the owners or not, but they didn't have much choice. I was the only one in town that weekend who actually knew what to do. Keep in mind I was fifteen and had neither a driver's license nor a third-class radio license required to operate a small 1,000-watt station like WPID.

A short time later, my parents took me to Atlanta where I took the test to obtain my radio license, and I then became a full-time employee of the station. I still drove to work each day for the next year illegally. I wasn't old enough for a driver's license.

This would be a good time for a disclaimer. I will mention much in this story that was probably illegal at the time, maybe still is. I will confess to ill manners, poor judgment and a lack of morality at that tender age that would embarrass my mother were she still living. I will take the liberty to blame all such behavior on my immaturity, and hope that all statutes of limitations have expired. I will mention many in this story who will go unnamed for obvious reasons. I don't want to implicate or blame anyone else for my brief foray into juvenile delinquency.

WPID's format was a hodgepodge of unlikely companions. During the week, from sign on at 5 a.m. until around 10 a.m. we played country music. From 10 a.m. to around 1 p.m. we played southern gospel. From 1 p.m. until 3 p.m. it was what we called "easy listening," and from 3 p.m. until sign off, which varied with the sunset each season, we played rock and roll. There were some days when I worked twelve-hour shifts and played all four formats.

During the school year I worked after school and sometimes the entire day Saturday and Sunday. In the summers, it wasn't unusual for me to work forty- eight to fifty hours a week. I was always a hustler and loved to make money. I volunteered for any hours that were available to me. I don't remember what I earned back then, and I'm sure it wasn't much over minimum wage, but it was a great job, carrying with it a bit of small town-celebrity.

My previous job was landscape maintenance. Actually, I don't think that term had been coined yet; we called it cutting grass. From the time I was thirteen, until I got the job at the radio station, I mowed lawns. I distinctly remember making on average about $60 a week at this enterprise. I only had one customer who paid me $5 and a couple more who paid me $4. All the rest were $2 and $3. That was a considerable sum in 1965 in terms of dollars. The work was hot and demanding with no days off.

You can see why a job in an air-conditioned room spinning records was so attractive. My regular shift was the rock show from 3p.m. until sign off each weekday, then usually, all day Saturday. I loved that time. It was my generation's music. Imagine getting paid at the tender age of fifteen to play rock and roll records in the afternoon.

On Sundays, we usually had local preachers from sign on to sign off, their only mission to save the unwashed of the community. Sometimes they taped the sermons in advance. Mostly they came to the studio for live programming. Some would bring musicians with them who would perform live as well.

WPID sat just off Highway 278, out east of downtown. It was a nondescript building nestled a hundred feet or so off the road. It was a very small building and archaic by studio standards of today. When you entered the building, you were standing in the office and reception area. A desk sat to the left but was only staffed when the owner's wife came in to create our program logs and bill our customers. A small door by the desk gave access to a restroom. Next to the restroom was another door, allowing access to the area behind the transformers that broadcast our signal. That was a rather noisy area, which also contained our teletype machine. A large fan was mounted on the outer wall which ventilated the cramped space behind the transformer to cool it.

On the other side of the lobby were two doors. The first was always locked. It opened into a room where the owner kept his tools. He was also our engineer and as such always serviced the equipment. The second door on that side of the reception area led into our studio. At the back of the studio was the door that gave access to our control room. The control room was the brain center. This is where the station operator sat to run the entirety of the station's broadcast. The entire front of the control room was glass and looked out into the reception area.

The station sat in a field of broom sage. That field always reminded me of the opening scene of the television show "The Lone Ranger," where Clayton Moore sat atop his horse in a field of wheat, gently swaying in the wind, a reference I assumed, to the show's sponsor, Merita Bread.

That field and the camouflage it offered was the genesis of one of the many pranks I am ashamed of. The station owned a large bugle-shaped speaker with a microphone that could be hung atop a pole or other vertical object to broadcast the voice of an emcee at local events, such as horse shows or store openings. The cord connecting the microphone and receiver to the speaker was about 150 feet long. One early Sunday morning, while having little to do at the station but connect remote broadcasts of church services through the station's board, my devious mind came up with pranks of which I am ashamed.

Across the highway from the station were several houses occupied by people who were mostly single and elderly. On bright sunny mornings, one of the men who lived there would come out on the porch and ensconce himself in a rocker. This gentleman had a fondness for beer and often would start his day with one of those beverages mid-morning on the porch. He often ended the day the same way, well after dark.

Early one morning before he came out for his morning session on the porch, a friend and I placed the large speaker next to the highway, concealed in the thick sage that grew there. The speaker was only thirty feet or so from the man's porch, which was just across the highway. The cord then was snaked back to the station, through the door, and the microphone hooked to the speaker. We could observe his porch from the desk in front of the large glass window at the front of the station. Once he was comfortable in his chair, I began to address him via the speaker. This speaker had a reverb feature that made its sound echo as if it was coming from outer space.

"Charles." (not his real name) He perked up. "Charles!" He rose from his chair and began to look into the shrubs that grew around the porch. He returned to his chair. "Charles, this is the Lord." We could not see his facial expression from this distance, but he appeared to get very still, his head tilting slightly upward as he looked toward the sky. "Charles, alcohol will be your demise. I am so disappointed in you." This prank went on for a few weeks. "Charles, children go hungry while you spend money on earthly pleasures."

Soon we heard from a neighbor, who had tried to lead Charles away from his debauchery, that he had come to her recently and told her he had heard from the Lord and given up his evil ways! Even though the motive was not honorable, maybe the end result was.

It seems that all my mischievous stunts occurred on Sundays when I had idle time. Another such disgraceful event that scared me to death was the result of our experimenting with alcohol just after turning sixteen. On Saturday nights, we would often visit a local bootlegger out on Highway 9. Our city was dry, so the easiest way for teens to get beer was through this local source. You would have to be introduced to the bootlegger through a friend who had gained his trust. It was a badge of honor when you finally had established trustworthiness and could go alone to the sordid source for your six-pack of sin.

Being young and inexperienced, we could only drink a beer or two at the most. We would hide the remainder, to be consumed the next weekend. The contraband was usually hidden in a ditch along a road or secreted in a field outside town. We couldn't leave it in the car or take it home. It might be discovered by our parents.

Early one frigid Sunday morning after such a Saturday night, a friend of mine had retrieved a partial six-pack from our hiding place and brought it to the radio station. I can't remember why, but he brought it in and sat it on the desk in the lobby. We were sitting there with the beer, not drinking it mind you, just reveling in the fact that we were somehow deceiving our parents and the local authorities by our ability to buy beer right under their noses in a dry town.

About that time, a preacher from a local Holiness Church pulled up in front of the station, arriving for his live broadcast from our studio. I panicked. Grabbing the beer, I frantically searched for a place to hide it out of sight from this man of God. I ran to the narrow space behind the wall that contained the transformers and the large fan that cooled them. I stuck the beer in a crevice beneath one of the transformers and ran back to the control room on the other side of the wall. The beer was now hidden beneath the transformer on my right, out of sight to visitors. To my left was a large window that looked into the studio so I could monitor whoever was performing there when doing a live broadcast.

I got the preacher into the studio, in front of the large boom microphone, and at the appropriate time, introduced him to start his broadcast. Fate intervened that morning. His microphone shorted out. I had no choice but to move him into the control room to use the microphone, at my control board, the only other available one in the station. I played music during the interval when we were moving him to the control room, showed him how to activate the microphone and told him I would be out front, and I could monitor him through the window that looked out into the reception area.

My friend and I then went out into the reception area. I stood in front of the large window, separating the control room from the reception space. I was nose to nose with the preacher across the glass from me as I carefully watched the meters that monitored all the equipment behind him.

A few minutes into his sermon, fate frowned upon me. I heard a loud explosion. Kaboom! My eyes frantically scanned the wall of meters, monitoring the broadcast transformers. All seemed normal. Then another kaboom! As I scanned the equipment trying to figure out what was wrong, I could see the alarm on the preacher's face. He tried to continue his sermon, but was confused. Was that the gun of an assassin he heard? Was he being attacked by the congregation across town that always challenged his interpretation of the Bible?

Through the glass, I silently encouraged him to continue, and mimed to him that everything was OK. At that moment, my eyes were drawn to the carpeted floor by the wall of transformers. A thick white foam began to ooze from beneath a panel there. A sharp aroma akin to green beans cooking on a hot stove began to permeate the entire radio station. It was then that reality struck! The beer I had hidden beneath the hot transformers were frozen solid from lying in the subfreezing temperatures that enveloped our community the night before. God was now punishing me for my untoward behavior through his laws of physics. The cans had ruptured and now spewed a pungent odor into the control room with the Holiness preacher who was just raging about the evils of alcohol and the abominable end that awaited those who partook!

I rushed back behind the wall of transformers where I had hidden the beer and began to extend a mop through a small vent to try and absorb the escaping vile liquid! Somehow, we got through the broadcast. Afterward, I again sinned, telling the preacher that an unimportant tube had burst and leaked its malodorous contents onto the floor. After he left, I was troubled by the fact that he somehow knew I was not honest. He probably prayed for my lost soul that very afternoon. At least he never mentioned the occurrence to the station owner.

Another such incident occurred on a Sunday when another Holiness preacher was on air in the studio. This time, I wasn't so lucky.

Remember, the studio was to the left of the control room with a large window through which I could observe the discourse of the guest. To the left of the window was the door that allowed access to the studio. To pass the time while a longwinded parson sterilized the masses, we would often gamble for pennies.

We would sit on the carpeted floor behind the door to obscure ourselves from the eyes of his holiness in the studio. One such morning, we played dice against that door. The studio was heavily insulated for sound. I had no idea you could hear dice rattling off the door. Such was the ignorance of my youth. This morning, the studio guest behind the door, was annoyed by the clicking sound that emanated from the door and covertly peered through the window. There he saw us heathens gambling while he spread the gospel. I am sure that equated to money-changers in the Temple in his eyes. Blasphemy!

It was strange how the most interesting things happened on Sundays at the station. There were two specific denominations in town, each convinced that the other was demonic, all as a result of their individual interpretations of the Bible. One group would be on air, and the other group would wait on them outside the station and attack them verbally when they left. You would have thought you were at a Saturday night wrestling match over at the National Guard Armory! Usually I could separate them. There was one time I had to call the police when I thought their differences were going to spill into physical violence. I never came to understand why these men, and women, who claimed great knowledge of the Bible, missed the greatest commandment of them all, love one another.

Other acts I committed were not as devious or cruel, but illegal or unwise just the same. There was a small grocery, or fruit stand as many called it in the day, directly across the street from the station. Garmany's was a "zippy mart"/ fruit stand. The store had a room built on the front of the enclosed building that was partially wood with the top part of the wall made of screen wire and then roofed. The floor of this space was for produce and was covered with fresh sawdust every week. I can still smell that wood pulp as I entered on a warm summer's morning, huge fruit flies buzzing the half-rotten produce. While we had a soda machine in the lobby of the radio station, Garmanys' was the closest place to get a snack. Early mornings, when no one was at the station with me, I had to improvise. It took me exactly three minutes and fifty seconds to jump from my seat at the control board, into my car, drive across the street, grab a honey bun, and drive back to the station; that is if I had backed my car into the lot that morning as I always did, so I didn't have to turn the car around before I made my assault on the market.

I had an assortment of a few records that played for five minutes and seven seconds to five minutes and twenty seconds that I cued up when I needed to make a run to Garmany's Market. My friends often told me they knew when I was making a grub run by the record that came on the radio. I rarely had to make these runs because friends were always hanging out at the station with me, except at 5 a.m. on a cold winter's morning, normal sign-on time.

We always signed on and off with a beautiful version of the song "Dixie." That was before political correctness skewered the way we were perceived. Those were simple times.

Though we often pranked others and found laughter in our mischievousness, we were an innocent generation.

I resigned my job at WPID in the early 70's when I left Piedmont to attend school at the University of Alabama. When I first arrived in Tuscaloosa, I majored in broadcast journalism and worked at the campus radio station. I soon burned out on broadcasting and changed majors. I guess I started in the business too young.

Still, some of the happiest times of my youth are tied to the radio station there, the escapades my errant friends and I committed with no malice intended. I hear that the Gladdens, who owned the station back then, now live somewhere in Florida. I owe them a huge debt of gratitude for giving me that job and for tolerating my often-childish behavior. I'm sorry for the escapades described here. I was a child and acted as a child.

Last I heard the station was still there and operating. I can't help but wonder: do those who now work there or those who own the place have any clue to the long-ago malefactors whose youthful innocence still haunts the place?

WPID

(l to r) Tim Webb and Stan Alexander

14

Fall

****

I love spring, but fall is my favorite season. In Northeast Alabama, we are blessed with four distinct seasons, but not to the extremes of our neighbors to the north.

Fall is a respite from the sapping heat and humidity of the Alabama summer, whose torpid days grind you down. My affection for the things October brings were birthed in me during my formative years and seeped into my soul where they still make me smile.

As the verdant hills that have been scorched by the oppressive heat of summer give way to warm and muted colors of fall, it feels good to be outside again.

Hunting was a thing I taught myself. My dad was not a hunter, though he did take me squirrel hunting once up on the mountain where the Piedmont Springs Hotel once stood. I never saw the old hotel except in pictures, but the remnants of its foundation and springs were still present when I went there as a child.

I learned to hunt with an old Winchester pump .22 caliber rifle my grandfather Posey had left me. I still have that gun. I also own an ancient single shot 12-gauge shotgun that belonged to my grandfather Webb, whom I never knew. He died when my dad was 2 years old from an illness that would be easily cured today. This gun is limber from use, the stock wrapped in tape. My dad told the story of how the stock was broken. Seems he was chasing a wounded rabbit through cotton rows after he failed to dispatch it with his only shell. He had to finish it off with a blow to the head, which cracked the stock.

Long before Dad ever gave me my grandfather's gun, I begged for a .410-gauge shotgun, less recoil for a young boy. I received one that Christmas. It was called a "youth" gun because of its short stock and was made by J.C. Higgins for Sears Roebuck Co. The single shot .410-gauge was the first firearm actually purchased solely for me, but there would be many more.

In jr. high school, the classrooms had parties at Christmastime, just before our holiday break. We drew names for presents. There was a $2 limit on the price of gifts and each name drawn would often have preferred gifts listed. It seemed the boys always requested shotgun shells, or English Leather or Canoe cologne. We were, after all, starting to notice the girls. Two dollars would buy ten .410-gauge shotgun shells at the Street and Mobbs store down on Ladiga Street.

I can't help but think of the terror that would strike in the student body and faculty today if a young boy opened a gift of ammo in his homeroom at the Christmas party. There would surely be a lockdown, and SWAT teams would soon be swarming the building

Though I lived in town, I was only a short walk from a copse of woods, a benefit small town living offered a young boy. Those woods provided habitat for small game. I think the first time I realized my mother loved me was when she agreed to fry one of the gray squirrels I brought home, all the while insisting they were nothing more than overgrown rats!

That same year, I was introduced to the thrill of rabbit hunting by Aaron Trammell, a friend of my dad who lived over on Fifth Avenue. Mr. Trammell was a tall man who walked hunched over a bit with a splayed, shuffling gait. His right hand was missing the thumb and first two fingers, lost in an industrial accident years before. Hands missing fingers were intriguing to a young boy.

My father and Mr. Trammell shared an affinity for cigars, usually Tampa Nugget Blunts. It was rare to see either of them without a short stub of a cigar clenched in the corner of the mouth. To my mother, those cigars were the next- worst thing to infidelity.

Mr. Trammell owned beagles, dogs built to chase rabbits. Their short legs and sensitive noses allowed them to enter the thickest undergrowth along fence lines, where rabbits tried to hide, then flush them out, where the chase was on.

We usually hunted property out in the country- Spring Garden, Forney- places with lots of pasture and rolling hills of piney woods and fence lines choked with old-growth briars and honeysuckle vines. Mr. Trammell seemed to know all these folks and have their blessing to hunt their land.

Mr. Trammell taught me how to "lead" the rabbit with my shot and to wait until the separation between rabbit and dog didn't endanger the dog. He also instructed me on "the circle." If my shot was errant, as it often was, I was to reload and wait. The rabbits almost always ran in a large circle and would return to the place where the chase began. In the beginning, after a hunt, we sometimes had to pick lead shot out of the dog's ears with a pocketknife. It took a while to get the lead just right.

Mr. Trammell hunted with a .16-gauge shotgun, a rarity even in those days. I remember its chromed receiver and how his two-fingered right hand flawlessly worked the gun. I hunted with my .410 "youth" shotgun. I don't think I've ever faced a more arduous task than hitting a small, speedy animal running a ragged pattern through brush with the small dose of shot that the .410 provided.

The dogs would scamper through the undergrowth, silent but for the rustling of the brush, until they struck a rabbit. Then they all fell in behind the foe; incessant shrill yapping echoed across the pasture and quickened my heartbeat.

We transported the dogs to our hunting grounds in a low trailer pulled behind his car. I can still smell that god-awful odor from the towels and hay that served as bedding in the bottom of the trailer, especially on a wet day after a hunt as the dogs, all lathered up from the morning chase, piled in for the ride home.

The hunt usually lasted into the early afternoon. Once we returned to town we drove over to what we called "Pepper Town," the black neighborhood near the old Bethune School. This was in the days of segregation. There we would stop and array the morning kill on the hood of the car and drive slowly down the street. This routine was repeated a couple of times to allow the word to get out. Soon residents came out on the street to pick out their dinner. We were paid fifty cents apiece for the rabbits. This more than covered the cost of our ammo. I don't think we ever kept and cleaned one of those rabbits for ourselves. That happened later.

That was about the time that I became a self-taught quail hunter. A friend who lived a few blocks away had access to his grandfather's bird dog, affectionately named Dixie. We took the dog into the woods adjacent to his grandfather's house and followed its circuitous path through woods and pasture until he suddenly froze, or "pointed", as I learned the proper vernacular. One of God's queer creations is a bird dog sensing a covey of quail and locking up, stiff, the only movement a slight vibration in his tail. His nose was always pointing in the direction of the birds. You could never see the fist-sized birds, hidden deep in the browning grass. Once Dixie pointed we raised our guns and walked in the direction of the birds until they "flushed," another quail hunting word, which means the birds would rise from their concealed refuge with a loud shudder made by their rapid wing thrust. Though I knew to expect it and had heard it dozens of times, that sound, like sudden thunder, always startled and thrilled me at the same time. Memories of the explosion of a covey of quail from a clump of sagebrush on an otherwise quiet afternoon in a fall wood still arouse in me the thrill of a hunt, unencumbered by the responsibilities adulthood would soon bring.

Fall was also known as "hog killing time." Weather was critical to this endeavor, as there were no refrigerated meatpacking rooms on the farm and few people acquired store-bought meat before refrigeration was commonplace. I now realize I probably witnessed one of the last hog killings my family ever conducted in the late 1950's.

As a very young boy, I remember traveling early one Saturday morning to my Uncle Dewey's farm in Cherokee County with my dad to participate in the event. When we arrived just before dawn, a fire had already been built under a large black cast iron pot.

The day before, I had witnessed the killing. The deed was done in a barn out behind our high school, on property I believe was owned by Mr. McGowan. The hog was unloaded on a cement pad enclosed in a narrow pen. A .22 rifle shot between the eyes made the death seem quiet and painless. Afterward the hog was hoisted by a block and tackle, then lowered into a large trough of boiling water. Once it soaked a few minutes, it was hoisted again and a man began to scrape the hair from the hog. Then it was disemboweled and awaited delivery to my uncle's farm early the next day.

My memory of those early childhood events, which were once so vivid, now seems foggy. A friend of mine has a theory that I subscribe to. He believes there is a little man in our head who, when we need information, runs to retrieve that information from behind hundreds of doors that store the data in our brain. When we are young, he is young. He hurries to gather information we ask for, retrieving it quickly and accurately. As we age, so does the little man. Now when we ask, he moves slower, he forgets which door is which. The doors are old and rusty, so they are harder to open. This is why, as we age, it takes longer and is harder to remember events in the distant past.

On the farm that morning, it seemed there were a half dozen or more people working on the hog. Each had a specific job to do. The smell of the crackling cooking in the pot soon pervaded the yard. Crackling is the skin, cooked in the large black pot to extract the lard, to be used for frying throughout the year. The crackling is then a crispy snack, nothing like the dry "pork skins" you buy today down at the local 7- Eleven. Quarters of pork were cut and carried to various tables where roast and hams were cut. Bacon slabs took shape at the cutting table. Defined parts were ground into sausage, with spices and herbs added; it was mixed and then packaged into neat bundles and wrapped in cloth for storage.

You have undoubtedly heard that "the only thing not used in the processing of a pig is the squeal!" I can avow to the truth of that statement.

Most of the meat that had no other purpose was carved from the carcass, boiled, and pressed with some sort of gelatin to form a loaf. It was then sliced as sandwich meat. We called it "pressed meat" or "souse meat". It has several other names, none of them flattering. I once saw an eyeball in a slice of pressed meat on my sandwich!

At the end of the day we came home with a trunk full of pork. At the time, we lived in a duplex beside my grandparents' house on Smith Street. Behind their house was an old "smokehouse." Maybe it was originally a smokehouse, or maybe they just called it that. It was mostly filled with garden tools, scrap lumber, canning jars and all manner of tin cans full of nuts and bolts. In a corner of the smokehouse was a large wooden box, shaped much like one a coffin would come in. The fact that it was stamped "U.S. Army" and had caliber and quantity size stenciled on its side gave away the fact it was an old ammunition box, probably scavenged from Anniston Army Depot, where my dad worked.

Dad carefully stacked the cuts of meat from the hog in this box, making sure each layer was covered in coarse salt before the next one went in. The next winter, this box would provide meat for our family's breakfasts and dinners. I can still smell the dampness of the old smokehouse as I would go there with Dad and watch him remove the lid, dig around in the salt for a piece of meat and return to the kitchen. I think that was where I developed my love of salt- cured country ham.

I still don't know why we stored meat that way. We had refrigeration by then. Maybe it was because there wasn't room for all the meat in the refrigerator and we didn't have a freezer. Maybe it was just a carryover from times past, a tradition to keep alive one more year, like drying fruit on a screen door between two sawhorses, or making sauerkraut in an old churn on the back porch. I witnessed those things too, but not much longer. Those labor-intensive chores soon gave way to modern appliances to do the work.

Over on the corner of 5th Avenue stood the remnants of what must have been a sizeable farm at one time. Suburban creep had pushed it up against itself, but large fields to the west, now subdivided, were clues its extent was once much larger.

We called it the McGowan place. An elderly man, at least he seemed elderly at the time to a young bunch of boys, lived just across the street from what remained of the farm. He was Mr. McGowan. His place consisted of a weather- worn barn, a garden patch and several acres next to this, which made up the syrup mill. On the corner, across from the farm, was the old field where we played minor league baseball in the summer. I played for the Vols, coached by one of the kindest men about town, Ed Spoon. My friends played for the Chicks, the Barons and several other ragtag teams.

Out in right field stood the National Guard Armory, a fixture in small towns back in the day. The armory served as the venue for the annual Fall Festival held each fall by the Frances E. Willard Elementary School, which sat just beyond the football field across the street.

It was always amazing to watch the armory morph into a sort of carnival at festival time. A skeleton work of pipes and wood was strung with burlap to create "booths" where the kids could play games such as "Go Fishing."

To this day, the most delicious sandwich I ever ate was a chicken salad sandwich only made in the fall and sold as a fundraiser at the school and at the Fall Festival. Someone had discovered the most amazing chicken salad sandwich recipe that ever passed the lips of a Southern boy. I don't know who had the recipe, but many women in the community were recruited to make the salad and sandwiches in the school lunchroom. The salad was slathered on white bread, sliced diagonally and wrapped in wax paper to be sold for ten cents each. (Plastic baggies were still far into the future.)

My wife got a recipe from somewhere a few years back that tastes just like that Fall Festival chicken salad sandwich that hooked me way back in the 50's. That recipe is now our secret, not to be shared.

The most intriguing thing to me about the armory had nothing to do with the Fall Festival. In a far corner of the building there was a large sandbox. The ceiling suddenly sloped down into the box at a severe angle. That part of the roof was made of steel. I soon learned that this strange contraption was an indoor shooting range for the National Guard soldiers. That was just about the most exciting thing I had ever seen. A place indoors where you could shoot your gun! Every chance I got I would dig in that sand and find lead that had ricocheted off the steel plate and fallen harmlessly into the sand. Once very symmetrical business ends of ammunition were now gnarled and deformed into irregular shaped lead balls.

At other times of the year, the armory would be converted into a gymnasium of sorts, where professional wrestling matches were held on Saturday nights. For a couple of bucks, you could watch fat men who worked weekday jobs at the mill or over in Gadsden at the tire plant transform into superhuman fighting machines with names like Chief Little Eagle, the Human Tornado and the Assassins, who wore masks that made them look even more ominous. I don't know that I ever saw those exact wrestlers in that armory, but many like them.

Sometimes the crowd was more entertaining to watch than the performers. Family members would turn on each other over loyalty to a particular wrestler. Grandmothers who sang in the church choir on Sundays used words of wrath, usually reserved for the pool hall, to dress down wrestlers they particularly loathed.

Early fall meant syrup- making time. Mr. McGowan's syrup mill would come to life just across the road diagonally from the armory. The sweet smell of cane juice cooking over an open flame whetted my appetite for the amber treat to come.

Mr. McGowan was a hard-working man. His appearance spoke to you from a distance. He wore high-topped brogan boots. His coveralls were clean and neat. He always had an old brown fedora pulled down close to his forehead. The syrup maker's face was thin and whiskered, edged with age lines. The cracked and calloused hands were a testament to many hard years. His countenance was one of wisdom, of how to scratch a living from that which the Lord provided.

The process began by pressing the juice from the cane. A large conical contraption sat near the piles of cane. An opening in its center exposed a mesh of gears: cutting teeth. Midway to the top of the crushing machine was a long arm made of steel that extended out about twelve feet from the machine. At the end of this shaft, a mule was harnessed to provide power. As the mule walked in a circumference defined by the limits of the shaft, it caused the gears to turn. Mr. McGowan sat on a rickety stool next to the revolving gears and fed the cane into the teeth. The cane was crushed and chewed and emitted a golden juice, which drained to the bottom of the grinder and was channeled through pipes to a tank at the foot of the cooker.

The spent cane fed out the other side of the mill where a worker gathered it and piled it outside the path of the mule. By day's end, the entire mill would be encircled by a wall of used cane.

Mr. McGowan sold a long cane to children in the neighborhood for a nickel. We boys snapped the sugar cane at its joints, to form short sticks to carry in the back pockets of our jeans. When we wished to indulge, we carefully peeled the hard, outer layer of cane to reveal the soft center, which we chewed to extract the sweet nectar. The outer layer was razor sharp, and would easily slit a finger if you weren't diligent at the task.

At the cooker, the process of syrup making got serious. The juice from the cane would be introduced to a large rectangular pan, maybe 4 feet wide by 9 feet long. Metal legs supported the pan. Beneath it a fire was built to cook the juice.

Once the juice was released into the pan, Mr. McGowan stood over it with a tool that looked like a small hoe with holes drilled into its blade. The pan was partitioned into compartments. As the juice cooked and began to thicken, it would be swooshed along to another compartment with the syrup hoe.

A tin roof that protected the process from the weather covered the syrup cooker. Once the process was started, it had to continue to the end. Another by-product of the process was heat, steaming up around the syrup maker. Mr. McGowan stood over the cooker, sweat beading his scruffy face, a rag in one hand to wipe his brow and the syrup hoe stirring in the other. The redolence of the sweet liquid boiling over the fire filled the air of a cool fall afternoon, wafting over the neighborhood, stimulating the appetite.

The amber syrup frothed and bubbled along its path, thickening as it ran toward the final compartment. There it cooled in preparation to be canned in silver cans with a lid that snapped on top. Those cans were stacked by the dozens in boxes nearby. Soon the syrup graced a golden brown buttered biscuit. The art of baking those biscuits was handed down from mother to daughter, much like the old wooden bowls and rolling pins they used in the process were handed down by the last generation.

One of those bowls graces the island in our kitchen today. The bowl was used by my grandmother and mother, who taught my wife how to make and bake biscuits. It mainly accommodates fruit these days. The rush of everyday life makes homemade biscuits a sweet treat for those leisurely mornings that are so rare today. Just as well, I guess. It's hard to find sorghum syrup these days, just like it is hard to find men like Mr. McGowan and Mr. Trammell, men who harbored deep knowledge of how to use God's gifts to create something special and fill a young boy's head with wonder that will always rest there.

McGowan Syrup Mill

McGowan Syrup Mill 2

15

Young's

****

The building sat just east of the intersection of Main and Smith Streets. Its front was made of rocks, small smooth stones like the ones that can be found in the creeks so common in the countryside.

Young's Filling Station is not to be confused with the truck stop out on Highway 278. Locals called it a fillin' station; the "g" was silent. Like all other stations of the day, it was full service, which meant an attendant not only pumped your gas but also checked your oil and the air pressure in your tires. Oh, and they cleaned your windshield too, squirting it with a fluid from a small, flat, white plastic bottle, not unlike the whiskey flask I saw old men share in the back alleys downtown. The attendants even carried them in their hip pockets the same way. Next, they would wipe the windshield with those reddish paper towels, none of those squeegees so common today. It wasn't uncommon for two different attendants to swarm around your car, all in neat uniforms with their name on the pocket. You didn't even have to leave your car to pay. I don't remember credit cards in those days, but you could charge it at Young's. The charge would be handwritten on a small pad the attendant carried in his shirt pocket, signed by the purchaser and later placed in a wooden drawer, alphabetically filed by last name. On the first of the month, people came in, their tickets were totaled, and they paid the bill.

Years later, as a teenager, when the old stone station had given way to a more modern structure on the corner beside it, I came in many a payday for Sammie Goss to add up my bill, pay, and start over again. Come to think of it, that was my early training of how to be responsible and how to budget. I learned that if you kept your promises and paid your bills on time, people all over town would give you a loan or let you buy on credit.

Sammy always greeted you with a smile. If you owned a business, he had the personality you wanted greeting your customers, always helpful, always customer service oriented. For a long time after I left Piedmont, when we came back to visit my parents, I'd stop by the station just to visit Sammy. His good nature always caused you to leave with a positive attitude. He was interested in where I was and what I was doing. It was a sad day for me when I read his obituary in the Piedmont Journal.

Young's was the nearest place to walk to get a snack for a young boy in late 1950's Piedmont. At least it was for me.

Outside on the left of the building stood two large tanks, up on stilts, I guess to give some sort of gravity flow to the fuel inside. I'm sure today's government regulations would require them to be buried in the ground, for our protection, of course. On the right side of the station was a cement pad with what we called a grease rack, a hydraulic contraption that lifted a car for easy access when changing the oil, or making repairs underneath. The rack was outdoors, mind you, the cement pad and the earth that surrounded it always soaked with oil, the essence of petroleum filling the air. The EPA would have had a field day there!

Once inside, you were greeted with a pleasing kind of clutter. The pleasant odor of new rubber emanated from the new tires and fan belts scattered about or hanging from racks on the wall. A glass-fronted cabinet held all manner of candy, and atop that stood one of those old wire racks with clips on it, each holding a bag of Tom's potato chips. But, the most attractive item in the station to a patron on a hot July day, was the icebox. It stood in front of the large glass window at the front of the station. It was a long metal thing, about five feet long and four feet tall, with a black rubber handle on top that was gripped to open the lid. It was painted fire engine red, and Coca-Cola was painted on its side in large white cursive letters. Inside was a double-walled tank made of tin. It was always full of water, slushy with ice. Buried up to their necks in the frigid water were all the popular drinks of the day in returnable glass bottles. You could usually make your selection by looking at the bottle caps peeping from the icy bath; there were Cokes, of course, but there was also Hires Root Beer, Upper 10 and Bubble Up, NuGrape and Orange Crush in those amber colored bottles. No diet drinks. That was long before we learned how unhealthy we were living, exposing ourselves to this sugary blight!

In those days, Coke bottles had the city where it was bottled engraved in the glass on the bottom. I still remember old-timers sitting around on lazy afternoons on wooden stools and wood-slatted chairs in the station, gambling. Actually, I don't think they considered it gambling. When thirst got the best of them, they would all draw a Coke from the icebox and compare the bottling site engraved on the bottom of the bottle. The one with the bottle the longest distance from Piedmont had to pay for all the drinks. Rome, Georgia, was the nearest bottling plant, so it was unlikely to be a loser.,

I didn't know Mr. M.V. Young. I saw him a few times around the place. He was bespectacled and wore a hat like my grandfather's. I knew he was a kind man. He just looked the part, carried himself that way. His kindness was later verified through a story my mom told me one evening before she passed away. She was reminiscing and shared a story from WWII.

Dad, like so many young men of the time, joined the Navy at the outbreak of the war. He was stationed in Oakland, California, awaiting his orders to ship out to the Pacific while Mom was back in Alabama with their newborn daughter. All operations in the military at the time were top secret. The sailors would not know until the last minute when they would ship out. During the wait, when activity picked up on the base, and Dad thought his orders would come soon, he wrote my Mom telling her he could leave in peace if he could just see his wife and daughter one more time.

Mom was on the next train to California with their new baby in her arms. Dad rented Mom a room in the home of an older couple just off base. Several weeks later, still no orders and money running low, Mom took a job in a shoe store to help make ends meet while the couple who ran the boarding house took care of the baby, my older sister, Kay.

Not long after that, my grandparents Posey, longing to see their daughter and terribly missing their firstborn grandchild, took the train to California, as well.

A short time after their arrival, Dad received his orders and was assigned to the USS Cabot, an aircraft carrier in the Pacific.

At that time, my grandfather determined it would be cheaper for him to buy a car and drive the family back to Alabama than to take other transportation. The only problem was that gas was rationed in those days because of the war and you had to have gas stamps to buy fuel. They bought the car, left Oakland, but became stranded in Texas when they ran out of gas and were without the stamps necessary to purchase more.

Desperate to get his family home, my grandfather called Mr. Young back in Piedmont. In a very short time, Mr. Young got enough stamps to my grandfather to get them home to Piedmont. I know there are kind people everywhere, but there just seems to be more of them in small towns.

Somehow, sitting here in the warmth of my home with everything I need and the means to get more, I feel a bit privileged, even spoiled by convenience and plenty. I know I will never know the deprivation and hardship my parents and grandparents experienced. It is so appropriate that Tom Brokaw titled his book about that time and those people "The Greatest Generation." They truly were. The things they endured, the things they did without, the mental anguish; and they did it all not knowing if they would ever see better days again. And what distinguished them most from my generation? They never complained.

Young's Service Station

16

Cars

****

Everyone remembers their first. Your first car is a ticket to freedom. No more lining up rides with friends or relying on parents to shuttle you; after all, many of the places you want to go, they don't need to know about. For the first time in your life, you have the means and ability to go alone, with alacrity, to places that those in authority over you might find abhorrent. Your universe had expanded exponentially.

Mine was a 1950 Plymouth Mayflower. While the model doesn't sound very exotic (and it wasn't), your first car is not the time to think about what is cool. You're free! You are suddenly independent of the rest of the world.

We nicknamed it the "Gray Ghost." It was the color of putty and had an interior larger than my first apartment. The Ghost had four doors, a manual transmission, and "three on a tree," in the parlance of the day, indicating a shifter on the steering column and a clutch next to the brake pedal. The engine was a six-cylinder and the body was made of real metal. You couldn't dent it with a bat. The bench seats were covered in a stiff gray cloth that did not show wear. The dash was metal, and a small knob in the center under the rearview mirror operated the windshield wipers, one speed. There was no carpet and no seat belts. Lights were dimmed by pressing a button on the floorboard next to the clutch pedal. Rubber mats lined the floor. The trunk was large enough to accommodate two of today's compact cars, and the lid would still shut flush with the bumper.

The car was a hand-me-down, originally owned by my grandfather. Though he died in 1958 when I was a young child, I still remember riding with him in that car on his daily rambles. The car was well worn by the time I received it. I don't remember how many miles it had traveled, but I'm sure the odometer had measured enough to circle the globe several times.

One of my all-time favorite teenage pranks was concocted in that car on a slow-news summer day. One friend would get in the trunk. A string attached to the lid would help him hold it down with one arm dangling lifelessly outside. We covered the limb with some sort of fake blood and let it dry. With three of us remaining in the car, we took turns driving up to local service stations, parking conveniently so as the "dangling bloody arm" could be seen by the proprietor. One of us would then go inside the station and ask the attendant if we could borrow a shovel.

That old Plymouth died one fall afternoon while I was leaving school and speeding down a hill on Fifth Avenue. I guess I missed a shift and over-revved the engine. The old six-banger breathed its last with a belch of blue smoke from the tailpipe and thunderous boom from beneath the hood. The old Gray Ghost had given up his.

My next car was a 1960 Plymouth Belvedere, a hand-me-down from my father. By now, it should be obvious, my dad was a Mopar man. That automobile was easily distinguished by the fins on each side of the rear of the car, that sprouted about a foot from the end of the car, and rose about twelve inches as they completed their span. Thus, it was nicknamed "the Batmobile." It was ugly like that. White with lots of chrome, an eight-cylinder 318ci engine with plenty of power, and a push-button transmission on the dash. Most people have probably never seen a transmission with that shifting mechanism.

By the time I turned sixteen, I was a bit embarrassed to be driving that car. My friends all had cool cars like '56 or '57 Chevys or '56 Fords. Pickups weren't yet in vogue for teenage boys. I eventually blew the engine in that car, too. It was a Sunday afternoon out in the Cherokee County countryside. The engine suddenly locked up. On the side of the old country road, I pulled the dipstick from the engine to see the dreaded oil and water clinging to its sides, the DOA announcement for the old three eighteen.

I was devastated. Sixteen and no wheels! I was almost suicidal by the end of summer. That is when I got the coolest car I would ever own. Ever!

In a used car lot on the corner of Center Avenue and Alabama Street, I spotted the sportiest car I had ever seen. It was a 1965 Ford Mustang 2+2. A Mustang marketed as a 2+2 had two rear seats, not standard on the regular Mustang. This dream car, was Persian Gold in color and a fastback in design, which meant it sloped from the top of the rear roof post down to the beginning of a short trunk lid. Under the hood was a 289 high-performance engine, one of the fastest and most durable engines to ever leave Detroit. Inside were bucket seats and a 5-speed shifter on the floor. Sitting in that car was akin to sitting in the cockpit of one of those dragsters we occasionally saw over at the Green Valley drag strip; you sat low to the ground like that with the shifter beside you at elbow height. The console and door squeezed you in tight, the view over the steering wheel much like that from a fighter jet. Oh, the sound of that engine when ignited! A low rumble from twin exhaust through competition mufflers, raising a ruckus as I pressed the accelerator, a combustible chorus perfectly tuned.

I needed my dad's approval and financing to buy the car. He tried his best to talk me out of it. He considered the Mustang a hot rod – and it was – and, he was afraid for my safety in that car, knowing my propensity for speed and trouble. He even offered to finance a brand-new Chevy Camaro I had looked at in Anniston, Alabama, but I had already been seduced by the beauty and muscle of that Mustang. He finally relented. I can't remember what I paid for the car, but I do remember my payments to Dad were thirteen dollars a month. I was expected to pay for the insurance, as well.

The Mustang had an interesting interior. The back seats fold down to make a flat cargo space in the back, much like a station wagon or van would today. At the rear of that space was a hatchway, which opened into the trunk. Perfect for pranksters! We went to the local drive-in theater with two passengers in the front and as many as we could cram into the trunk. That was a small trunk, not like a full-size car. But, unlike a full size, the trunk did not have to be opened to remove its contents. Perfect to smuggle your friends into the drive-in: Open the hatch once inside, and they could stealthily crawl to the front.

There was a night in late summer when we tried to defraud the old Midway Drive-In near Anniston in this fashion. Just before entering the drive-in, three passengers entered the trunk. Three was the maximum that could fit in the space, and it left little room for oxygen. After paying at the entrance, we entered the lot to find a space and a speaker. In those days, drive-ins had wired speakers on posts at each parking spot. You would park, then hang the speaker on your rolled-down side window facing into the interior of the car. It was often a challenge to find a speaker that worked! Those who remember drive-ins back in the day may remember how each parking spot was a bit elevated in the front and lower in the back; I presume this was to position the car at an angle to improve viewing. As I was driving through the lot I decided to cross over one of those spots rather than go to the end of the row and enter a new row the proper way. The low-slung carriage of the Mustang hung up on the elevation and the rear tires were slightly off the ground. I began to spin the tires trying to rock the car back and forth over the hump. Dust and exhaust fumes filled the air…and also filled the trunk. It must have appeared as if a small tornado had touched down. Several of the workers in the concession stand saw our dilemma and came to help. As they arrived at the car they heard the choking sounds coming from the trunk. Busted! I had to open the trunk immediately or risk suffocating my friends. I felt fortunate when the management asked us to leave and never return, rather than call the police. Young and foolish.

That reminds me of another night at a drive-in, one of my first with a girl. As the movie got to the romantic part, I asked the girl if she would like to get in the back seat. Her response: "No, I'll just sit up here with you."

As I recount my many foibles as a youth, I realize why my parents worried when I was out alone with no parental supervision. This also explains to my children why, when they turned 16, I told them to remember, "you can't B.S. a B.S.er. I had pulled every prank they could imagine and their high-jinks were thwarted.

Our mischievousness knew no end. Weekend nights would find most of the teens in town "cruising." The normal route took us from the corner of Center Avenue and Ladiga Street east, past the post office, through the mill village and past the mill itself, around the Hilltop station on the curve and to the Dari King. Circling the Dari King, we would retrace our route to downtown and turn right at Bud Kirk's Service Station and go north past the pool hall to Frady's Coffee Cup, which again would be circled to repeat the trip. Sometimes we would extend the route past the Coffee Cup and turn around in the large parking lot in front of Joe Lively's grocery store. That was before Lively's moved to Ladiga Street.

When gas and the means to purchase such was in short supply, we parked somewhere along that route and sat like hoodlums on the hood and trunk. Popular spots were along Ladiga Street, at the Dari King, or at Hilltop Grocery and Gas Station, later run by Coot Powell. Sometimes there were so many cars parked at the Hilltop, it was impossible for customers to access the gas pumps or find a place to park while they shopped. If the outdoor lights flickered a couple of times, that was Coot's signal to clear the space. He never had to ask twice.

As kids at the time, we were fortunate to have merchants in town like Coot Powell at the Hilltop, the Grissoms, who ran the Dari King, and Clyde Pike at the YMCA. They not only tolerated us, but also looked out for our safety and well-being. Another reason I was blessed to grow up in a small town, especially this one.

If your car was parked unattended while you cruised with friends, you might have been the victim of our mischief. I was amazed to learn that a stem of a green weed could be used as an electrical wire to conduct current, at least until it became dry from the heat passing through it.

Cars in those days had distributors that provided spark to the cylinders to ignite the fuel there and...well, if you aren't mechanical, it doesn't matter. Suffice it to say that the distributor had a wire that fed electricity to it from the coil, and then distributed it to the cylinders to ignite the fuel to power the car. We would lift the hood of unoccupied cars, remove the distributor wire, and replace it with a blade of a green weed… just tuck one end of the weed into the top of the distributor and the other into the coil.

When the unsuspecting owner came back, the car cranked and ran for a minute or two until the weed was exhausted of its moisture. The engine died and did not restart. If the owner was not mechanically inclined, he never diagnosed the problem. We always placed the original coil wire in the glove box of the cars, which were never locked in those days. That way, when we passed the owner stranded later in the night, we could tell them to look in the glove box. We were degenerates, but not cruel.

In fact, we tried to be nice. At the time, there was a resident of Piedmont named John Kinzalow, who walked everywhere he went. I don't know if he couldn't drive or just didn't have a car. John was a pleasant sort, always smiling. His hair was coal black and he sported a mustache. His shirt pocket was always full of cigars. Rumor had it that John would take a tape recorder to every Little League baseball game played at the YMCA and record the action. I'm not sure why.

John was the fastest walker I've ever known. His legs were a blur as he walked down Ladiga Street. Any time we saw him walking, we rolled down the car window and asked if he needed a lift. His response was always, "No thanks, I'm in a hurry!"

There were other colorful characters in our town. A tall, wispy black lady would walk the streets holding a staff. We called her "Watusi" because she seemed over seven feet tall. She walked everywhere, mumbling as she went…not that there is anything wrong with that. I never knew what she was saying, too afraid to get close enough to hear.

Then there was the "Goatman." The Goatman was an infrequent visitor, usually passing through in the summer. He arrived in an old, beat-up wagon with wobbly wheels pulled by a team of anywhere from 11 to 30 goats. You could hear, and smell him coming from a distance, the pots and pans and other junk hung from the wagon's sides clanging with the movement. He often camped for the night in the field out by the radio station, WPID. Locals gathered a short distance from his camp, bathed in the smoke from his campfire, to observe and hear him occasionally preach. You didn't want to get too close; the essence of unwashed goats and man were overpowering.

The Goatman was dressed in goatskin clothes and sold postcards of himself by the wagon with his goats. He claimed to have traveled all over the United States, but at that time he mainly traversed a few Southern states.

I later learned that his given name was Charles McCartney. He was originally from Iowa, but in later life called Georgia home. He was said to have inspired a character in Flannery O'Connor's work after she saw him encamped in her home state. Old man McCartney died in Georgia in 1998, at the age of ninety-seven.

But I digress. Another prank was to take a potato and push it against the tailpipe of a car until its flesh was firmly embedded in the exhaust. Once the car was cranked and the exhaust began to build up with no way to escape, it would choke the engine. The remedy was to either get out of the car and physically remove the potato from the exhaust, or to floor the accelerator to create high RPMs, which ejected the potato from the exhaust. Of course, you had to recognize that you had been pranked to know what the cause of the engine problem was.

That happened to me once. As I left the Dari King headed

back to the center of town, the engine began to choke. I immediately knew the cause, geared down, and floored the gas pedal. In the straightaway just past the mill, the potato was quickly ejected and the Mustang suddenly reached 70 miles an hour – in a 30-mph zone. At the same time, I met the Piedmont city cops heading in the opposite direction. They quickly did a 180-degree turn, and suddenly blue lights filled my rearview mirror. I think this was the only time I ever talked a policeman out of a ticket, though I have tried many times. After explaining the prank to him, I convinced him I had been the victim of some misguided youth in the city and he laughingly let me go. I just know he was impressed with this trick and would one day use it on a fellow officer!

Another time I was not so lucky was when I was clocked at 75mph in a 50mph zone in Heflin, Alabama, racing to a high school football game. Good `ole boy politics were around even then. When the officer wrote the ticket, he said I would have to go to jail and await the judge on Monday, (it was only Friday night,) or he could take me to the Justice of the Peace's home, where I could pay my ticket. I was young and naïve. We followed the policeman to a large house in the town, where we were escorted into a dimly lit room to be greeted by an ancient, obese lady reclined in front of a television. She was introduced and then the cop explained the charge. She gave us the same option the policeman had earlier: Cash only. I don't remember the price of the ticket, but it could not have been much. Between three of my friends and me, we scraped up enough to satisfy her. She gave us a handwritten receipt from a store-bought receipt pad. Nice little scheme these devious town officials had.

While this car was truly a muscle car built for speed, I only raced it twice: once legally and once illegally. The unlawful one took place on a late afternoon at Stewart's Bridge. Stewart's Bridge was named for a family who once lived nearby. A county road with little traffic and a long, straight stretch of wide asphalt, it served as an unauthorized drag strip for the denizens of the area.

A friend of mine, a few years older than me, had ordered a custom-built 289 engine from Holman Moody, the official racing contractor for Ford at the time. It came complete with racing headers, etcetera, but was built to be street legal. Knowing the capabilities of my Mustang, the friend asked me to drag race him just to see how his car performed. I would not race a car built by a racing company with my factory-built car. That would be humiliating. He convinced me that the race was to simply see how his car performed against a factory-built car, assuming his custom engine would outperform mine. I finally relented. Just the two of us drove out to the bridge one afternoon for the contest, no one else would know the result. He had removed his mufflers and the car sounded like a dragster. To my surprise and to his disappointment, my car won the quarter mile race by two car lengths!

The legal race took place at the Green Valley drag strip near Gadsden. With confidence that this car really was special in its ability to produce short-range speed, a friend and I entered it to race at the Valley. The car had four races in an elimination-type competition that night and won all four to win its division. A beautiful trophy was a testament to the car's ability. The trophy had a tall, silver figure holding a tire with wings above its head. That trophy, once so important to me, now collects dust in a box somewhere in our basement.

I never raced the car in competition again, partly from fear of being caught by my parents and losing my privilege to drive it, but mostly from the fact that I knew the special speed the car possessed. I guess you could say I retired from racing undefeated.

My dad and I lay on the cold cement floor of our basement

installing more clutches in that car than I care to remember. That was about the only mechanical work it ever required, though it was daily put through its paces. There are many more stories I could tell about that Mustang and the wonderful times I had during our time together, but I will let them remain "my memories."

When it came time for me to go to the University of Alabama in Tuscaloosa, I sold the car. I decided it would be too expensive to drive there. I purchased a very modest six-cylinder Plymouth Valiant from a relative to drive to school. I was too embarrassed to drive it around town – after all, I had an image to maintain. The young man who bought the Mustang almost wrecked it as he left the house, squealing the tires and fishtailing the car down Anniston Avenue. It was obvious he had never sat behind that kind of power. I heard he did wreck the car sometime later, totally destroying it, though I am not sure. I like to think it is still out there somewhere, well kept in a garage and occasionally driven, or dust-covered in some old barn waiting for me to find and rescue it. Those cars were rare. Seems they only made the 2+2 that one year. Pontiac had a 2+2 GTO before Ford introduced that one and Ford was sued to change the name, I'm told.

I looked on the internet the other day for cars from this vintage for sale. There weren't many. I found one in good condition for sale...for $150,000! There was a beat-up one that was only $50,000. Mind you, this car sold new in 1965 for under $3,000. It is extremely rare to see one of these cars on the street. There just aren't that many left. I do occasionally see one on display at a car show.

Strange how I don't remember being that emotional the day I sold it. My priorities had changed. I was headed in a new direction. About a year or two later I began to miss the car, as if it had some human quality, like a friend I no longer saw. Today that memory has grown into full-blown nostalgia. The people, the times and places and the events associated with that car take me back. Take me back to places forgotten by time, things changed by progress, and finally, one of my favorite chapters of life before adulthood. We were privileged.

The Mustang and me

The Goatman

Dari King

Dari King

17

Fireside

****

The jagged orange flames licked at the dried hickory wood, and the heat warmed me. The cherry-red coals seem alive, shimmering in the firebox like rubies in the sunlight. Errant embers pop against the fire screen, trying to escape the heat, then settle back into the ashes.

The flames now seem to speak, like a soft whisper in the wind. The sound of the fire slowly consuming the wood is the only sound here on the patio late at night.

A fact in this chapter of my life is that I never sit beside a fire that doesn't elicit memories from deep in my soul of people and places I have shared a fireside with over the years. Perhaps it is because some of my happiest moments were spent with my father and cousins somewhere in Calhoun or Cherokee counties cutting firewood.

My earliest memories of cutting wood go back to a time when I must have been about 11 years old. Much younger than that, and I could not have pulled my end of the crosscut saw. I'm sure my dad, on the other end, did most of the work. That was before chainsaws, I guess. If they had been around, my dad would have had one.

I'm sure no one uses these old saws anymore. Too labor intensive. They have been relegated to the antique category. I still see them occasionally at a trade day event or at craft shows. Those at the latter usually have the working part of the saw painted in some scene of farm life or the like.

We were up near the old city dump in Piedmont. I can still smell the acrid odor of the garbage smoldering in the late afternoon, a noxious vapor that hung across the landscape and pierced the shade of the trees where we worked.

We were a few dozen yards into the woods that surrounded the dump. I don't know if that was public or private land, but either way I am sure we were breaking the law in some way by cutting wood there. We only cut one tree at a time. That was all our old-fashioned tools allowed. We cut the tree into sections and loaded it on a trailer we pulled behind the car. Back at home the arduous task of splitting the wood took place near our woodpile on the edge of the alley that skirted the side of our house on Montview Road.

We drove steel wedges into the ends of the wood with a sledgehammer. They had to be placed just right to make the wood split. On larger logs, it was sometimes necessary to use two or more wedges. I learned very quickly you didn't try to split sweet gum logs. They were stringy and would not split apart. Your wedge could be driven deep into the wood and lost forever, unless you just burned the log and got the wedge out of the ashes, but that caused the steel to lose its temper. Later, we used splitting axes, a strange cross between a sledgehammer and an axe.

I remember playing with friends on those piles of firewood after it was split. The essence of the freshly cut wood with the sap seeping out in the cold afternoon air was very pleasing to me. Still is. The wood had to dry for many months before it was ideal to burn. Green wood gave off lots of heat but was hard to ignite.

As I grew older, after college, when my wife and I had moved to Birmingham, I drove up to Piedmont on weekends and my dad, cousin and I, drove Dad's truck to my uncle's farm. There, another cousin joined us, and we spent the better part of a Saturday somewhere up on Weisner Mountain felling trees.

By this time, one of my cousins had acquired a gasoline-powered wood splitter. It was almost like cheating. You would place a fire-stick length log under this large wedge that was mounted on a vertical hydraulic driven rod. One pull of a lever and the log would instantly be split. That took a lot of the hard labor out of our task and certainly sped up the process.

But it really wasn't about time, it was the sheer joy of being in the woods with your buddies. It didn't matter how long it took. We could all have afforded to buy firewood by that time. There was just something about sitting in front of the fireplace back in Birmingham and burning wood we had cut and dried the year before, remembering the fun we had cutting it and knowing from where it came.

It was more of a ritual of fall than it was a chore. One of the deepest feelings of accomplishment is waking up with a sore back and sore muscles and looking out at a stack of wood you yourself cut, split and transported home.

Sitting around the fire tonight, now many years distant from those days, I remember the day we cut a tree down on my daddy's truck.

We were up in a pasture next to a tree line. The ground had a gradual slope to it from the field up into the woods. We had backed the truck up close to the wood line so we wouldn't have to carry the heavy wood far. By now we owned chain saws.

One cousin and I were cutting trees behind the truck. My father was about 50 yards away on the same line cutting trees in clear view of us.

As I contemplated felling a rather large tree, my cousin and I discussed the arc the tree might take as it fell. I was convinced if I notched the tree on the far side the tree would fall away from the truck, which sat about 10 yards behind us. My cousin was afraid it would fall toward the truck, which sat in the middle of its path to the ground.

Young and foolish and wanting to prove my point, I began to work on the tree. As the chainsaw ate its way through the wood, it soon became apparent that my cousin had correctly predicted the path of the fall. It was too late when I discovered that he was right. The tree began to lean back toward me and I quickly moved away.

A sudden loud snap and the tree fell, centering my dad's truck lengthways. Once the tree was down, we could no longer see the truck. It was completely buried beneath the green branches of the tree. The only sign that a truck was beneath the huge fallen tree was the sun glinting off a silver radio antenna, the tip just peeking through the foliage.

I was suddenly nauseous. How stupid was what I just did! If I had simply moved the truck it would not have mattered which way the tree fell. But now…

I looked down the way to where my dad was working. When he heard the horrible sound of wood crushing metal, he stopped and looked our way. It was a long look. Then he slowly turned and went back to work on the tree he was sawing.

That was typical of my father. Once something was done that was irreversible, he wasted no time fretting over it. That was just one of my many foibles he tolerated over the years. My dad rarely got emotional. He was a very tolerant man when it came to overlooking other's mistakes, especially those of his children. He didn't worry about that which he could not change.

I later learned that those were the behaviors of a good leader; he could be both kind and tough, and he knew when to use both. Dad always used humility when your mistakes were embarrassing and you knew so. Often, the only thing Dad would say was, "What did you learn?" I now call that stupid tax!

My cousin and I immediately set to determining the damage to the truck. We cut away limbs for what seemed like an eternity until all that was left of the tree was the enormous trunk. The bigger end of the trunk rested across the tailgate, forming a depression about 12 inches deep. The remainder of the trunk centered the cab where it made a slightly less deep impression. Several of the limbs we trimmed away had made small dents and scratches, much like hail damage.

When we finished clearing the limbs, I looked up and my dad was standing there surveying the damage. The only thing he said was "You best run on down to the farmhouse and get a heavy hammer," which I did.

By the time I returned, dad and my cousin had cut the trunk into several smaller pieces and rolled it off the truck. With the hammer, we beat the roof of the cab back up so we could drive it home.

Years earlier I had camped on that mountain with my dad and two nephews. They were both young, maybe early teens. It was their first outing with my dad in the woods. We had a huge fire that night, the firelight making creepy shadows on the surrounding woods. If we walked away from the light of the fire we could see the dim points of light of a farmhouse far below on Forney Road. We slept that night in sleeping bags in the back of a truck and on the ground next to the fire. Waking up the next morning, all our gear was covered with a rime of ice. We quickly rekindled the fire and prepared breakfast.

Those two boys are all grown up now, both doctors. One is an extreme outdoorsman, attributing the fact to his visits to Piedmont as a boy and the hours he spent in the woods.

We had two fireplaces in my childhood home, one in the den and one downstairs in the unfinished basement. We alarmed the whole neighborhood one winter's evening when the fireplace caught fire and spewed its built-up creosote on the roof like an erupting volcano. We probably would not have known about it until it was too late had a neighbor not seen it when arriving home. A knock at the door and we were all out of the house like rats fleeing a sinking ship! Someone called the fire department. By the time they arrived, dad had controlled the flames with a water hose. They finished the job.

We all knew about creosote and how it can build up in a fireplace over time. Today we call a chimney sweep when we fear this dangerous occurrence. Back then we did the job ourselves. I doubt there was a chimney sweep in the state back then!

The problem was the result of some bad information. My dad had been told by a reliable source of course, that burning aluminum cans in the fireplace when you had a hot fire would rid the chimney of the combustible residue. We had done that on a few occasions. I still don't know if that is true or not, but it certainly didn't work for us. These days you can buy chemicals at the hardware store for this, or better yet, in larger cities you can find a chimney sweep.

The fireplace in our basement became an iconic place to sit on a cold and rainy day in January. Over the years, lots of stories and lies were told by numerous people who gathered there.

At Christmas each year, Dad cooked a fresh ham in that fireplace over very low heat. Seems like it would take the better part of a day and night. Sometimes Mom would finish it in the oven and apply her homemade barbecue sauce at the end.

Fresh hams are hard for me to find today, but I can special order them from most stores. Back in the day, Mom would pick one out at H.J. Morgan's grocery. He always stocked them during holiday season.

Mom made a coleslaw that dressed those barbecue sandwiches up fit for a king. We would always add a dip of sauce to the finished ingredients. Lord, I can taste it now!

Through the years, I sat by many a campfire at hunting camp, from Alabama to Georgia to Colorado. One of my favorites was down in South Georgia, at a colleague's camp situated on a beautiful lake. It was just him and me that night; the rest of our entourage was arriving the next day. He and I had prepared a wonderful meal of grilled steaks that night. Now, totally sated, we built a roaring fire, one of the largest I ever remember. We enjoyed an adult beverage or two in the firelight. It was a cool evening, but not yet cold. The trees surrounding the cabin on the edge of the lake were dressed in Spanish moss that gently stirred in the wind. The sky, full of stars, sparkled like gold. The glow of the fire was reflected in the lake and made for an almost surreal setting.

Overcome with the serenity of the moment, we decided to get in the canoe and paddle out into the darkness of the lake and look back at the campsite lit by the fire. The scene from the lake that night, the quaint cabin backlit by the huge fire, the trees framing it all, is indelibly pressed in my memory. From the lake, the whole scene looked like a movie set, all lit up for filming some night scene, total darkness surrounding that one scene lit only by flames from the wood we had gathered that day.

I have often thought of what a beautiful painting that scene would have made that evening. We were in fact artists that night. We had built that scene and then sat in the wonder of the beauty it created.

When traveling with my job and working in Calhoun County, I would often visit a cousin who lived in the country just outside Jacksonville, Alabama. This was one of the same cousins I had cut firewood with over the years. He became one of my best friends and running mates at the time. Sadly, he is gone now.

We both shared an interest in the outdoors, hunting and fishing. He had a large garage out behind his house. We called it "the shop." Strangely, it always seemed in a state of organized clutter. Every imaginable tool could be found there, and my cousin could find it. Sometimes a trailer or old car occupied a space while he worked or welded on it. In one corner was a wood-burning stove. Many a night we whiled away next to that fire. Sometimes neighbors would visit and a poker game would break out. Strange how thinking about the place some twenty-five years later I can still smell it, always redolent of greasy tools and a damp cement floor.

Fishing rods stood tangled together in one corner. On warmer days, we used them to pull huge catfish from the pond just a few yards from the garage. At the end of a hot summer's day he'd feed the catfish food from a drum in another corner. The quiet stillness of the pond would suddenly erupt as the catfish roiled the surface to fill their mouths with the pellets and quickly dive back into the coolness of deeper water.

My cousin had a fireplace inside the house too. He had

installed a firebox insert into the space. This firebox had a large glass window in its door through which you could see the flames. Once the fire was started, you could close the airtight door. The cast iron heater was much more efficient than an open fireplace, emitting heat from its iron body but making the wood burn more efficiently. While it was certainly practical, it did not have the same character as a fireplace.

Years later, we built a fire pit at our lake house. There was a fireplace inside the house, which we used on bitterly cold nights. It became very apparent to me, out in the countryside, you were exposed to a whole new world. The sky was so brilliant with celestial bodies that it was magical! With no artificial light from street lamps, flashing lights from antenna towers, neon strobes and such, God's perfect light, as it was meant to be, bathed nature in a beautiful aura. The woods around the cabin almost glistened. The lake reflected the beauty of the sky, creating a serene place unknown to those who have never lived outside the city. The only sound was natural too, the cicadas, the gentle rustling of the leaves, as a warm summer wind tickled the tree branches.

Have you ever smelled a fire built of alligator juniper? If you've ever stayed at an Arizona resort and sat around one of the outdoor fireplaces so common there, the fragrant wood they burn is usually alligator juniper. The cedar like fragrance of this wood is similar to mesquite wood, which is also burned there and used to smoke meat. The mesquite is so dry it burns quickly and is usually burned with other hardier wood to last longer. Alligator juniper gets its name from its alligator-like bark. These trees are ubiquitous in the higher elevations of Arizona. The female tree has berries that are used like an herb in food.

There is something very distinct about the fragrance of this wood that you won't forget. Kathy and I last sat by one of these fires when we attended the national championship game in

Scottsdale, Arizona back in 2015.

I was reminded of another night in the past, at this same resort, when the managers in our company sat around such a fire and ceremoniously burned the rank sheet that showed our team finished dead last in the country that year. Afterwards we had to look at the person to our left and tell the group something we admired about that person. We were lubricated that night, so it was a funny affair.

There have been many other occasions where I've enjoyed campfires abroad. There was a night in the Jordanian desert when Kathy and I sat with friends in a Bedouin tent and sipped strong tea around a fire just a few miles from ancient Petra.

One evening in Kinsale, Ireland, in County Cork, this same group enjoyed Irish folk music performed by locals around a stone fireplace in a quaint pub near the mouth of the River Bandon. Here the river dumps into the Atlantic. On May 7, 1915, just eleven miles off shore, German U-boats sank the Lusitania. Eleven hundred and ninety-eight people lost their lives in this tragedy that caused the United State to enter World War I.

A few years ago, after my dad had passed and mother was living with us in Birmingham, we sold their home in Piedmont. Dad would not let me sell the house while he was living. He always thought somehow, he would be able to go back and live there someday. It wasn't to be.

When a buyer was found, we had very little time to clean out the house. My nephews and brother-in-law went there with a large trailer one weekend to gather what we wanted to keep from the basement. There was a treasure trove of tools, most anything you could ever need. We loaded everything we could carry into the trailer and two pickup trucks. Much was left for the auctioneer who came in a few days later to sell the rest.

After everyone had left I stood alone in the basement, now clear of all the clutter that once defined it. I looked at the old fireplace one last time before leaving. I knew I would never see it again. Because of my faith, I do know I will see many of those who gathered with me there over the years. I had grown up in that space from 3rd grade until I went off to college. Now it was time for someone else to create memories in this house.

I looked at the concrete wall painted white at the foot of the stairs leading up to the house. There on the wall, in crude pencil marks, was the record my dad had created each time the grandkids visited, each mark showing the date of the visit. Their growth through the years was indelibly pictured there. My dad so enjoyed those visits, especially when we lived far away, but there was always sadness in his countenance when we left for home.

Tonight, as I sit alone by the fire in the early hours of morning, memories of those people and places overwhelm me. The dog-irons in the fireplace were handmade by my father. They have rested in every fireplace I have ever owned. The memories are so vivid. They bring such pleasure. Most of the people in this story are gone now. Some live so far away we rarely see each other. But fireside on a cool evening, I can go back there, if only for a little while, to the memories that were recorded so long ago in such a simple way. Life is good.

Fireside

Tim H. Webb

EPILOGUE

It had been a hot week in August when I decided to take a trip back to Piedmont as I finished this volume. Rain pelted the windshield as I drove into town, a cool 70 degrees was refreshing, for a change. A heavy fog hung over Dugger Mountain, like a diaphanous drapery, cobwebbed like that.

As I drove around town, I could only find two businesses that still existed from the old days. Young's service station, the new stripped-down model that replaced the old rock building, stood at the corner of Main and the Anniston Highway. On the southwest corner of that same intersection sat the OK Tire Store, once run by Hubert Masters. I'm told both these businesses are still operated by offspring of the Young and Masters families.

The houses I remember from childhood are still standing, and most look the same. Driving by places where old friends once lived brought back memories that took place there over 5 decades ago, though none of those houses are occupied by the same people. Driving around my old neighborhood on Montview Road, across Anniston Avenue and turning on 5th Avenue, I saw all the houses of my parents' friends. The home places of Aaron Trammell, Chuck Stewart and the Fields family, all look the same but now are the homes of another generation. It's sobering to know that the people who once drove those streets, worked in the shops out back, mowed the grass and stopped whatever they were doing to help a kid find his errant baseball are all gone.

Just last week I heard of the death of Ray Floyd, a longtime neighbor, who stood in my parents' kitchen with tears in his eyes the day we loaded them up to move them to Birmingham. People there truly loved their neighbors. Sometime after moving my parents to be closer to us, I went back to check on their house. I found a neighbor mowing the lawn. It was Mr. Hart from just up the alley. I wanted to pay him. He refused. He replied, "They always kept the place looking so nice, I just wanted to keep it that way, should they ever be able to return." He's gone now, too.

Downtown I found a bar and restaurant on Center Avenue, just across from where the pool hall used to be. Beer for sale, legally, in Piedmont!? There was no name on the business that I could see, but the Rocky Mountains on the neon Coors sign shining through the front window gave it away.

I didn't see any faces I recognized as I drove around town. I was shocked to see what was left of the old cotton mill. What was once the city's largest employer has been razed except for the first-floor brick wall that runs along the curve on East Ladiga Street. When I turned the corner to drive by the YMCA, I saw what used to be the interior of the building exposed, lying in heaps of scrap metal and broken up concrete; the old loading dock overgrown with creeping vines. It looks like one of those photographs of German factories years after they were bombed in WWII. The old Lawtex/Springs plant on 5th Avenue no longer produces bedspreads, curtains and comforters. Plants like these all over the South became the victim of cheap Chinese and Taiwanese labor.

All the ball fields around the YMCA have been replaced with grass and playgrounds. I understand there is now a nice athletic compound just out of town. The pool has been covered over, seeming to symbolize the burying of the past. The Hilltop and the old Dairy King, once gathering places of all the kids who could drive, sit forgotten, their darkened windows a sign of something important gone forever.

While I think the current mayor is doing his best, you have to work with what you've got. I was impressed to hear a story that seems to define the current mayor, Bill Baker. On a recent holiday a resident called him at home to report a dead animal in the street in front of her house. Rather than call street department employees, who were off that day, the mayor drove to the house himself to remove the carcass. Whether you agree with his politics or not, that is a servant centered leader. This is how my generation was raised in this mill town. Take responsibility.

As I left town headed home, I drove south along Highway 9, enjoying the beauty of Dugger Mountain and smiled at the long ago visions I had triggered by my visit to my hometown. I remembered old friends, most of whom I have lost track of. A quote seeped into my mind, the author remains unknown to me:

Home is not a place...*it's a feeling.*

Made in the USA
Columbia, SC
18 November 2018